An Absence of Shadows

An Absence of Shadows

Poems by
Marjorie Agosín

Translated by
Celeste Kostopulos-Cooperman,
Cola Franzen & Mary G. Berg

WHITE PINE PRESS · FREDONIA, NEW YORK

WHITE PINE PRESS

10 Village Square, Fredonia, New York 14063

716-672-5743   Fax: 716-672-4724   E-mail: wpine@netsync.net

Publication of this book was made possible, in part,

by grants from the National Endowment for the Arts,

the New York State Council on the Arts,

and Wellesley College.

Cover: Liliana Wilson Grez, *Proposition 187*, 1996. Color pencil on wood, 18" x 24"

Book design: Elaine LaMattina • The text of this book is set in Goudy Old Style

Printed and bound in the United States of America

1 3 5 7 9 10 8 6 4 2

ISBN 1-877727-92-X

LIBRARY OF CONGRESS CATALOGING-IN-PUBLICATION DATA

Agosín, Marjorie.
    An absence of shadows / poems by Marjorie Agosín ; translated by Cola Franzen and Celeste
Kostopulos-Cooperman. —1st ed.
        p.   cm. — (Human rights series ; 6)
    ISBN 1-877727-92-X (paper : alk. paper)
    1. Disappeared persons—Argentina—Poetry. 2. Human rights—Argentina—Poetry.
    I. Franzen, Cola.   II. Kostopulos-Cooperman, Celeste.   III. Title.   IV. Human rights series
(Fredonia, N.Y.) ; v. 6.
    PQ8098.1G6A6 1998   98-37956
    861—dc21   CIP

ZONES OF PAIN

An Absence of Shadows

In memory of
Reneé Eppelbaum,
founding member of the
Mothers of Plaza de Mayo

Preface

My parents were married in Santiago de Chile on June 19, 1948. It was winter in the Southern Hemisphere. The rain was incessant and my mother's bridal dress became a sea of water from the sky! "It's a symbol of good luck," the rabbi said. "You will shed no more tears." In that same year, the United Nations Declaration of Human Rights was ratified so that tears would never again be shed in the wake of horrors like Nazism and Fascism.

Yet millions of tears have continued to be shed by the innocent victims of war, and especially by women and children. The rapes perpetrated by neighbors, the disappearance of children and the ransacking of homes forced these victims to become refugees and deprived them of their language, which is where memory and identity reside.

The U.N. Declaration of Human Rights documents the way in which humans should live, and yet as we near the twenty-first century, the destructive forces of nationalism and ethnicity continue to torture, kill, and prevail. One is born with human rights, and thus one is sacredly connected to all living things. When human rights are violated, so is the sacredness of our world. Neighbors who rape and murder neighbors, civil authorities who torture the children of friends are among the darkest shadows on our century. Civilians have become tyrants in what was once the province of the military, and in these wars there can never be victory, only ashes and a sea of tears.

Poets, whose role is economically unimportant in the 20th century, have become the voices that ask for compassion for the voiceless victims. They see beauty amidst the horror and find the courage to speak against injustice. They see the urgent need for accountability. My poems acknowledge those voices muzzled in dark and silent torture chambers, especially the voices of women and of children who were forbidden to sing and denied the opportunity to grow knowing the soothing touch of a parent or to simply gaze, unafraid, at open horizons.

I, like many of my generation in Latin America, have been displaced. Exile became a way of life, and you had to choose to either remember or forget. When my family and I left Chile, we took nothing of importance but a bag of earth and a few photographs. Although our emigration was less arduous than that of others, and my father had a new job awaiting him in North America, I have always felt a very deep and authentic kinship with the displaced people of the world.

Poetry has saved me from oblivion, from forgetting, and from walking the earth as a stranger. Although I came of age in a foreign country speaking a foreign language, I witnessed from afar the brutality of the Pinochet dictatorship that mutilated an entire generation of people just like me. The poems in this volume commemorate the 50th anniversary of the U.N. Declaration of Human Rights. Two of the sections were previously published as individual books. *Zones of Pain*, first published in 1988, attempted to give a voice to women who were imprisoned and silenced forever. It also celebrated the journey toward light of those who choose truth and justice over evil. The second, *Circles of Madness*, published in 1992, pays tribute to the gallant mothers of the Plaza de Mayo. These brave women gathered each week in the Plaza de Mayo in Buenos Aires to bear witness to the absence of their beloved family members, who had been "disappeared" along with thousands of others by the military government in Argentina between 1976 and 1983. Their refusal to let the world forget these atrocities is perhaps the most important women's human rights statement of this century in the Americas.

The new poems represent once again reflection and a struggle to understand what happens to societies as they forge new democracies. These works also explore what happens to communities of people who remain silent bystanders while others are terrorized and murdered by those who hold power without democratic consent.

Some of my own Chilean countrymen have betrayed not only their dreams of democracy but also their own souls. The former dictator is senator for life, an assassin is portrayed as a venerable grandfather and torturers walk freely in the streets of Santiago without fear or remorse. Their victims still live in fear and, often, shame.

An *Absence of Shadows* asks essential questions concerning societies in the throes of democracy. It also acknowledges the valiant role of women who defied the brutality of Fascism and the brutality of silence. Octavio Paz has said that poetry is an act of both solitude and communion. These poems were written in the solitude of a foreign land in the language of my homeland. They were created with the belief that the horror stories of others are very much our own.

Fifty years after its ratification, the U.N.Declaration of Human Rights continues to be our most important legacy. Yet poetry, too, has its place: it demands accountability and truth. It is my hope that readers will share with me a sea of hope, a poetry of witness that honors the U.N. Declaration of Human Rights, a poetry that believes that memory, courage and the right to remember and give voice are also human rights.

Fifty years later, my parents are still married and the U.N. Declaration of Human Rights continues to remind me of laws, true covenants and rings of hope.

—Marjorie Agosín
Ogunquit, Maine
Summer 1998

An Absence of Shadows

Una ausencia de sombras

Translated by
Celeste Kostopulos-Cooperman

Una ausencia de sombras

I.
Más allá de las sombras
donde mora el viento
entre los extraños,
en las lejanías del reino
nublado del miedo,
están ellos
los desaparecidos
entre las sombras
en los intersticios del sueño.

II.
Es posible oírlos entre
las ramas muertas,
entre ellos se acarician y reconocen,
han dejado las luces encendidas de la foresta
y las velas del amanecer y el amor.

III.
Más allá de la
provincia
hay una ausencia,
una presencia de sombras
y de historias.

IV.
No les temas,
acércate a ellos
con la paz de la ternura,
sin rigor sin fuegos fatuos.
Más allá de la sombra
en las trizaduras
del viento,
moran ellos y nosotros
en el reino de la ausencia.

An Absence of Shadows

I.
Beyond the shadows
where the wind dwells
among strangers,
in far away kingdoms
clouded in fear,
the disappeared
are among the shadows
in the intervals of dream.

II.
It's possible to hear them among
the dead branches,
they caress and recognize each other,
having left behind the burning
lights of the forest
and the tapers of dawn and love.

III.
Beyond
the province
there is an absence,
a presence of shadows
and histories

IV.
Don't fear them,
approach them
with gentle peacefulness,
without vehemence and senseless rage.
Beyond the shadows
in the streaming gusts
of wind,
they and we dwell
in the kingdom of absences.

Tú

Tú que vanamente
hiciste de tu lengua
un mapa del olvido;
tú que en vano
enmudeciste ante
la memoria de estrellas huecas.

Ahora
sólo vives para recordar,
y en los memoriales vencidos
rescatas el nombre de tus padres, buscas sus ojos,
sus lenguas,
los campos
donde murieron vacíos,
tus padres,
tu hermana menor
en el más hondo desierto.

Tú me pides a mí
que los recuerde
que sean el
paisaje
entre mis manos.

You

You who vainly
made your tongue
a map of forgetfulness;
you who vainly
kept silent before
the memory of hollow stars.

Now
only live to remember,
and in defeated memorials
you rescue the name of your parents, you look
for their eyes,
their tongues,
the fields
where they died empty,
your parents,
your younger sister
in the deepest desert.

You ask me
to remember them
so that they will be the
landscape
between my hands.

Preguntas

No reposaré en mis preguntas,
el recuerdo se perfila como una viajera errante.
Abuela, cuéntame de aquellos campos
donde los niños se vestían con el tatuaje de las
estrellas.

Insisto en preguntar
de aquel tiempo donde yo no estuve,
de aquellas estaciones sin calendarios,
de aquellas praderas donde las mariposas
parecían muertas en un silencio de
nieves muertas.

Abuela, quién era Julia?
Dónde estaba tu casa?
Quién se quedó con tu jardín de lilas
con tu canasta de fresas?

En vano las preguntas,
como una piel agrietada,
recorren la historia que se desvanece,
la historia de un tiempo sin tiempo
donde los hombres
cercaban a los niños
en un jardín de alambres
con sus estrellas doradas
dibujándose en la luz
de las mariposas.

Abuela, cuéntame de tu memoria
cuando la noche era un vértigo nublado,
cuando no les temías a los fantasmas
pero sí a los hombres
de las noches.

Questions

I will not rest easy with my questions,
memory's profile is like a vagabond woman.
Grandmother, tell me about those camps
where children were clothed in tattoos made of
stars.

I insist upon asking
about a time that I did not inhabit,
about those seasons without calendars,
about those meadows where butterflies
seemed dead in the silence of
frozen snow.

Grandmother, who was Julia?
Where was your house?
Who ended up with your lilac garden
and your basket of strawberries?

In vain the questions,
like cracked skin,
traverse a history that vanishes,
a history of a time without time
where men
imprisoned children
in a barbed-wire garden
with their golden stars
sketched among the light
of the butterflies.

Grandmother, tell me from your memory
when the night was a vertiginous cloud,
when you didn't fear ghosts
but the men
cloaked in darkness.

Otra vez

Otra vez las ociosas,
hablando de los desaparecidos:
por algo habrá sido
¿no es cierto?
ya han pasado de moda
nosotros los chilenos
somos todos amigos.
¿Es Ud. chilena?
fueron poquitos los muertos
unos mil no más
nosotros los chilenos
somos buenos para el olvido.

Otra vez las ociosas,
marchando con sus trajes de viudas negras
me ponen nerviosa verlas transfiguradas,
en las rondas secretas de la muerte
yo no tuve la culpa.
me escondía cuando se los venían a llevar
en la frondosa noche de los veranos.

El hijo de mi vecino es policía.
yo soy tan sólo el vecino
de ese señor.
no supe nada del asunto.
los escuchaba.
eran ruidos de pájaros chirridos.
eran como si la piel se transformase en otra piel.

Y otra vez estas señoras
con sus vestidos rojos de la muerte
con gorriones en sus cabellos
no se cansan de bailar,
buscan refugio en la verdad
y buscan abrazos y nuevos hijos para amar.

Once Again

Once again the women linger,
talking about the disappeared:
it must have been for something
isn't it true?
they are no longer in vogue
we Chileans
are all friends.
Are you a Chilean?
few died
a few thousand, no more
we Chileans
are good about forgetting.

Once again the women linger,
marching in their black widow dresses
they make me nervous seeing them transfigured
in the secret circles of death.
It wasn't my fault.
I hid when they came to take them away
in the luxuriant summer nights.

The son of my neighbor is a policeman.
I am only the neighbor
of that man.
I knew nothing about the matter.
I heard them.
They were sounds of shrieking birds
as if my skin had transformed into another's skin.

And again the lingering women
with their red dresses of death
and sparrows in their hair
do not tire from dancing,
they search for sanctuary in the truth
and look for embraces and new children to love.

Nosotros los chilenos somos amigos
matamos a unos pocos
les quemamos unas uñitas
los tiramos al río
les quemamos los testículos y los pezones
pero era una guerra
así me lo dijo el
policía vecino
yo no sé nada del asunto
los años pasan
las palabras estorban
aquí no ha pasado
nada
los chilenos somos amigos
hasta en el perverso secreto de
las malas muertes.

We Chileans are friends
we kill a few
we burn some fingernails
we throw them in the river
we burn testicles and nipples
but it was a war
that is how my neighbor
the policeman described it to me
I don't know anything about the matter
the years pass
words disturb
nothing
has happened here
we Chileans are friends
even in the perverse secret of
wicked deaths.

Obediente la niña

Obediente la niña
con sus zapatos lustrados
el blanco vestido del orden.
Obediente la niña
saluda al general
que le rebanó las uñas
al hermano menor
que quemó los pechos
de la hermana mayor.

Obediente la niña
sonríe, hace las reverencias
apropiadas
y toda turbada gime
cuando un soldado la
llama hermosa
y roza su mano de guerra entre
sus piernas adormecidas.

Obediente la niña vive
porque en un país de niños obedientes
los fantasmas jóvenes aparecen
en días de luz salvaje
para secuestrar a las niñas desobedientes,
a las gitanas perdidas entre los bosques
de luz y sombra.

Obediente la niña
se acerca al soldado
y lo besa con temor
es el soldado que incendió
los libros de su casa,

The Obedient Girl

The obedient girl
with the patent-leather shoes
and starched white dress.
The obedient girl
greets the general
who sliced the fingernails
of her younger brother
and burned the breasts
of her older sister.

The obedient girl
smiles, makes the appropriate
curtsies
and moans completely flustered
when the soldier
tells her she is beautiful
and rubs his hand of war between
her lifeless legs.

The obedient girl lives
because in a country of obedient children
young ghosts appear
on days of savage light
to kidnap disobedient girls,
gypsies lost in the forests
of light and shadow.

The obedient girl
approaches the soldier
and kisses him with fear
he is the soldier who burned
the books of her house,

10 que rajó sus vestidos rojizos
10 y jugó con los candelabros de
4 plata y sangre.

38

7 La niña obediente
2 no habla
9 es una muñeca dormida
5 y se deja hacer
90 10 como si su cuerpo fuese un país   símil
7 de viajeros oscuros.

28

who slashed the crimson dresses
and played with the candlesticks of
silver and blood.

The obedient girl
doesn't speak
she is a sleepy doll
who surrenders herself
as if her body were a country
of obscure travelers.

Noche

I

Más allá de la noche,
entre los umbrales cristalinos del sueño,
ellas las viajeras
caminantes con pies de ríos,
viajeras por los pozos errados de la muerte,
buscan, preguntan,
cantan, sollozan
les preguntan a los rosarios
por los días del retorno,
regresan en el secreto sueño de la noche
a la casa de la noche,
a la casa sin palabras,
a las camas pobladas de los muertos
y sus guirnaldas de violetas.

II

Más allá del día,
se preparan las viajeras,
buscan, preguntan, sollozan.
En el pueblo, todos las conocen
pero les huyen
y ellas insisten en esa dulce tranquila
pregunta:
¿Ha visto a mi hijo?

III

Buscan, cantan, sollozan
les preguntan a los rosarios
a las brujas de las comarcas,
que ofrecen hierbas para el olvido,
y regresan a la casa secreta de la noche,
a la cama poblada de muertos,
a la casa sin lengua,
al idioma austero de la ausencia.

Night

I
Beyond the night,
among the crystalline thresholds of dream,
the women travellers
with feet sprouting rivers
wanderers through the erroneous wells of death,
search, inquire,
sing, weep
and ask the rosaries
about the day of the homecoming,
return in the secret dream of night
to the pitch-black house,
to the house without words,
to the beds populated by the dead
and their violet garlands.

II
Beyond the day,
the women travellers prepare themselves,
search, inquire and weep.
In the town, everyone knows them
but runs away
and they insist upon that sweet, peaceful
question:
Have you seen my son?

III
They search, sing, weep
and ask the rosaries
and the witches of the district,
who offer herbs for forgetting,
and return to the secret pitch-black house,
to the bed populated by the dead,
to the home without a voice,
to the austere language of absence.

El Presidente

Todo vestido de blanco,
despojado de las gafas oscuras
del sable dorado,
el general, todo de blanco,
desfila por la ciudad
de los muertos y los vivos.
Nada interrumpe su paso.
Marcha diligente entre la sombra de
los muertos.
El general no escucha el quejido
de madres viudas.
El general no se detiene ante
las orejas danzarinas en los pavimentos.
Nada mancha el traje blanco.
El sol del verano temeroso,
encandila sus ojos demasiado azules,
sus párpados inmóviles.
El general desfila entre los muertos,
pretende que están vivos.
Sólo el general se pasea por su patria,
un jardín de huesos,
un parque de madres buscadoras,
una patria en busca de un nombre.

El general se viste de blanco,
una perversa mancha rojiza
emana en su sable dorado.
El general se viste de blanco,
nieva en la ciudad
este verano en la patria de los muertos.

The President

All dressed in white,
without his dark glasses
and golden saber,
the general, all in white,
parades through the city
of the dead and the living.
Nothing interrupts his movement.
He diligently marches among the shadows of
the dead.
The general doesn't hear the cries
of the widowed mothers.
The general doesn't stop before
the dancing ears on the pavement.
Nothing stains his white suit.
The fearful summer sun,
blinds his too bluish eyes,
his frozen eyelashes.
The general parades among the dead,
pretending they are alive.
Only the general marches for his country,
a garden of bones,
a park of searching mothers,
a country searching for a name.

The general dresses in white,
a perverse red stain
emanates from his golden saber.
The general dresses in white,
it snows in the city
this summer in the country of the dead.

Reneé

–A la memoria de Reneé Eppelbaum

Todavía ella se acerca
murmura, suspira
por ese rostro,
por esa fotografía,
que ha estado muerta
por más de tres decadas.
Ya no busca
en la oscuridad ahuecada
de las ciudades
ya no va a la plaza.

Tan solo se acerca
sobre esta fotografía
y le dice que
se la llevará de paseo.
Recogerán castañas,
hojas muertas y vivas,
y que de pronto
la mostrará,
no para preguntarles por ella
sino para decir
que ésa era una hija
que no pudo
ser
que no pudo recoger frutillas.

Reneé

—In memory of Reneé Eppelbaum

She still approaches
murmurs, whispers
for that face,
for that photograph
that has been dead
for more than three decades.
She no longer looks for her
in the hollow obscurity
of the cities.
She no longer goes to the square.

She just approaches
this photograph
and says that
she will take her for a walk.
They will gather chestnuts,
dead and living leaves,
and suddenly
she will show her to others,
not to ask them about her
but to say
that she was her daughter
who could not
be
who could not gather seedlings.

El Salvador

−para Eva Asher

Me cuenta Eva
que es de El Salvador,
del territorio manchado
de la guerra.
Si, El Salvador
donde los vivos y los muertos
se recogen
con las pérfidas uñas de la
muerte.

Dice Eva, que
es una judía en El Salvador,
que sólo hay 60 judíos en
El Salvador.
Ellos también se han ido
porque el olor a humo de
El Salvador es
como el humo de Treblinka.

No quieres pensar
en un jardín de muertos
porque sería regresar
a Auschwitz.
Ya ves, la
historia regresa
en la memoria de los
vivos,
que son los guardianes
de los muertos.

El Salvador

—for Eva Asher

Eva tells me
that she is from El Salvador,
from the stained territory
of war.
Yes, El Salvador
where the living and the dead
gather
with the perfidious fingernails
of death.

Eva says that
she is a Jew from El Salvador,
that there are only sixty Jews in
El Salvador.
They also have left
because the smell of smoke in
El Salvador is
like the smoke in Treblinka.

You don't want to think
about a garden of the dead
because that would be like returning
to Auschwitz.
As you can see,
history returns
in the memory of
the living,
who are the guardians
of the dead.

Eva
me cuenta del Salvador
y yo veo en sus brazos
la sombra de la ceiba,
las urdimbres del maíz
y su destino de refugiada y prófuga,
de judía errante salvadoreña.

No queda nadie en El Salvador
me dice ella.
Nadie,
ni siquiera los judíos.

Eva
tells me about Salvador
and in her arms I see
the shadow of the ceiba tree
the strings of corn
and her destiny as a refugee and fugitive,
as a wandering Salvadoran Jew.

No one is left in El Salvador
she tells me.
No one,
not even the Jews.

Dominga

—Para las víctimas de El Mozote & para Claudia Bernardi

Mucho estuve adormecida entre los
escombros.
Los aullidos
de los otros
desvirtuaban mis oídos.
Allá, muy cerquita.
allá no más,
Yo parecía estar muerta,
entre ellos,
los niños y sus trajecitos del domingo.
Luego me supe viva,
y les cuento más lo que
vi y lo que oí.

Soy Dominga Faustino
del Mozote,
del Salvador.
Mi lengua quedó arropada en el silencio,
apapachada de miedo.
Por muchos días, o tal vez años
no encontré palabras.
Yo también
me había muerto con ellos
y pensé que esto era el cielo:
una tierra muy gruesa
y oscura.

Entonces, alguien me despertó.
Eran los ecos de las niñas
muertas

Dominga

—For the victims of El Mozote & for Claudia Bernardi

I was asleep for a long time among
the rubble.
The howls
of the others
rang in my ears.
There very close
just over there,
I seemed to be dead,
among them,
the children and their Sunday outfits.
Then I discovered myself alive,
and I will tell you more about what
I saw and heard.

I am Dominga Faustino
del Mozote,
from Salvador.
My voice remained clothed in silence, cuddled in fear.
For many days, or maybe years
I did not find the words.
I also
had died with them
and thought that this was heaven:
a very thick and
dark clump of soil.

Then, someone woke me.
It was the echoes of the
dead girls
the trees blushed

y los árboles se sonrojaron
también con todas esas
risas.
Estoy viva.
Tuve frío.
El miedo era una navaja cóncava.
No llegaron los ángeles
como el cura nos había asegurado.
Pero yo viví.

Les quiero contar que mataron
a los niños, a las mujeres
a las mujeres con niños adentro.
Se las llevaron más allá del cerro.
Vivas se las llevaron y
de pronto se oían gritos.
Las enormes fogatas en
todos los cerros
llevaban los vestidos
rojizos de la muerte
y de la vida que luchaba.
Los soldados se ponían los zapatos de los
muertos y bailaban con ellos
y se llevaban las joyitas de lata.
Así eran estos jóvenes.
Eran niños del bosque salvaje.
No los vi pero sentí
el replicar de sus salvajes palabras.

Por muchos años no salí de estos árboles.
Parecía que los días eran como
noches
y yo no tenía ni días
ni memoria.

with all their
laughter.
I am alive.
I was cold.
Fear was a concave knife.
The angels did not arrive
as the priest had assured us.
But I lived.

I want to tell you that they killed
children, women
and women with children inside.
They took them beyond the hill.
They took them alive and
suddenly screams were heard.
Enormous bonfires in
all the hills
carried the crimson
dresses of death
and of a life that struggled.
The soldiers put on the shoes of
the dead and danced with them
and took off with the tinsel jewels.
This is how these young men were.
They were children from the wild forest.
I didn't see them but felt
the echoes of their savage words.

For many years I didn't leave these
wooded lands.
The days seemed like
nights
and I didn't have light
or memory.

Era mucho antes de los estampidos
y los incendios de la carne mía.
Ahora comienzo a recordar.
El recuerdo es tibio como la sangre,
sangre de sacrificios vacíos.

De pronto,
todo se hizo como un pozo azul de
noche mala
Alguien llamó a la puerta
y les cortaron la lengua,
como si fuera rosa del jardín.
Yo me arrastré
porque al golpearme me
puse sonámbula, malherida.

Pensaba si todavía
había gente buena por los alrededores
y tan solo me habían dejado a mí morir
sola o vivir
sola, porque daba
igual eso de ser o no ser,
estar o ser sonámbula sin memoria,
sin otoños claros.
Allí entró el sueño de la muerte
entre los pastizales,
pero me han encontrado
para que les cuente.
He vuelto a amarrar mi telar de sueños
adentro llevo una hija.

It was well before the stampedes
and the burning of my flesh.
Now I begin to remember.
Memory is tepid like blood,
the blood of vacant sacrifices.

Suddenly,
everything became like a blue well in
an evil night.
Someone called at the door
and cut out their tongues,
as if they were garden roses.
I dragged myself
because while beating me,
I became dazed, badly wounded.

I wondered if there were still
good people in the region
and if they simply had left me to die
alone or to live
alone because it was all
the same to be or not to be,
to be or exist dazed, without memory,
without clear autumns.
Death's sleep penetrated there
among the pasture lands,
but they have found me
so that I will tell you.
I have begun to tie up my dream bag
I carry a daughter inside it.

El miedo

El miedo
anidaba
como un murmullo
extraviado en las
gargantas secas.
Nada decíamos,
éramos un arpa carcomida,
pequeños gemidos
en la proximidad
de todas estas perversas
distancias.

Fear

Fear
nested
like a murmur
lost in
parched throats.
We said nothing,
we were like decayed harps,
little moans
in the proximity
of all these perverse
distances.

El miedo II

El miedo ya no era esa presencia contínua que se complacía en apropiarse de nuestro entorno, de nuestras miradas que buscaban en la escasa transparencia del aire. El miedo estaba guardado en las crisalidas recónditas de la memoria, era un parpadeo de ojos que acechaban sin espacio ni tiempo preciso. A veces pensé que ya no éramos un país de poetas sino un país de miedosos que después del largo tiempo del insomnio solapado, después del tiempo de las palabras muertas, salíamos del olvido. Queríamos recordar la utopia voladora de los sueños pero teníamos miedo ante nosotros, miedo ante los gestos insólitos de la fraternidad, miedo ante el abrazo no clandestino, el abrazo como un gemido de felicidad. Pero teníamos miedo no ante el general con sus largas capas de veranos blancos, teníamos miedo ante lo que nos estábamos convirtiendo, una nación muy sorda ante la memoria, una nación temerosa y perdida entre las cordilleras mudas, entre las maderas mudas. Todo alrededor nuestro insinuando el gran silencio, el tiempo de las mentiras y el ocio.

Fear II

Fear was no longer that continuous presence that took pleasure in appropriating our surroundings, our gazes that searched in the meager transparency of the air. Fear was kept in the deep crysallis of memory; it was a flickering of eyes that peered menacingly without space or precise time. Sometimes I thought that we were no longer a country of poets but a country of cowards who after a long time of deceitful insomnia, after a time of dead words, came out of oblivion. We wanted to remember the soaring utopia of our dreams but were afraid; we feared ourselves, feared unusual fraternal gestures, feared the open embrace like a sigh of happiness. But it wasn't the general with his long white summer capes that we feared. We feared what we ourselves were becoming: a nation deaf before memory, a fearful and lost nation amid the mute cordilleras, amid the mute forests. Everything around us insinuating a great silence, a time of lies and idleness.

Declaración humana por los
derechos del niño

Nosotros los niños
del universo
exigimos el derecho
a jugar en
columpios y balancines
milagrosos.

Nosotros los niños
exigimos el derecho
a mirar al cielo,
como una mariposa color violeta,
o como una raya de encaje colorido,
el cielo sin polvos amarillos
ni helicópteros verdes.

Nosotros los niños
exigimos el derecho
al tiempo del ocio,
al descanso en una alfombra de hojas verdes,
al derecho al sueño de las hadas
y los buenos presagios.

Nosotros los niños
exigimos el derecho
a la leche,
al chocolate,
a los sabores del alma.

Nosotros los niños
exigimos el derecho a la memoria
del maíz,

A Declaration of Human Rights
for Children

We, children
of the universe
demand the right
to play on
swings and miraculous
seesaws.

We, children
demand the right
to look at the sky
as a violet-colored butterfly,
or a ray of colored lace,
a sky without yellow dust
or green helicopters.

We, children
demand the right
to spare time,
to rest on a carpet of green leaves,
the right to fairy-land dreams
and good omens.

We, children
demand the right
to milk,
chocolate,
and the flavors of the soul.

We, children
demand the right to the memory
of cornfields,

al tiempo sin premura
como un cuerpo que descansa y ama.

Nosotros los niños
exigimos el derecho
a los libros,
a los lomos azules que los cubren,
al alfabeto,
a la brisa de las palabras,
al amor.

Nosotros los niños
exigimos el derecho
a la paz y no a la guerra,
no más volantines carmesíes,
tan solo un cielo limpio,
una mano que acaricia
y no ata.

Nosotros los niños
exigimos lápices,
cuadernos azules,
columpios para llegar al cielo.

a time without haste
like a body that rests and loves.

We, children
demand the right
to books,
to the blue bindings that cover them,
to the alphabet,
to a breeze filled with words,
to love.

We, children
demand the right
to peace and not war
no more crimson-colored rockets,
only a clear sky,
a hand that caresses
and doesn't tie.

We, children
demand pencils,
blue notebooks
swings to reach the sky.

Napa

Como en la frescura del amor,
como el sueño de una boca sobre
otra boca,
los campos se deshicieron en
un verde alivianado
después de las lluvias.

Tu boca sobre mis labios,
tus labios sobre mi boca.

Más allá de nosotros
los campos después de la lluvia
y las flores amarillas,
el pasto verde,
el musgo enamorado
y esa pasión asombrosa
sobre el amarillo extasiado.

Tu boca sobre el césped,
mi cabello sobre el amarillo
del paisaje.

Tú y yo mudos
ante la felicidad.
Te dije que después de las lluvias
las flores amarillas
son un manto de cosas sagradas.
Cabalgamos sin premura;
no habían rutas
ni destinos.

Napa

As bountiful as love,
as in a dream of one mouth
over another,
the fields dissolved into
a light green verdure
after the rains.

Your mouth on my lips,
your lips on my mouth.

Beyond us
the fields after the rain
and the radiant yellow flowers,
the green grass,
the beloved moss
and that wondrous passion
over the enraptured yellow.

Your mouth on the grass,
my hair on the yellow
landscape.

You and I silent
before happiness.
I told you that after the rainfall
the yellow flowers
are a mantle of sacred objects.
We galloped without haste;
there were no routes
or destinies.

Tus manos
conocidas y ajenas,
siempre
tus manos
sobre los labios,
cual travesías de palabras
silencios entre el paladar de las estrellas.

Repetía tu nombre
y el nombre de las flores amarillas,
salvajes pequeñas.
Yo también te dije
que te amaba
como quien ama las cosas de la niñez
donde moran las palabras primeras.

De pronto,
nublados ante la belleza
los vimos
inclinados cabizbajos oscuros
más allá del abismo.
Los trabajadores de los viñedos
tenían la piel nublada
y el corazón en calma;
eran los hombres del pueblo extranjero.

Mexicanos recogiendo las uvas
en fronteras prestadas.

Ellos no veían las flores amarillas
ellos no sentían los colores del amor.
Ahí estban ellos
los hombres mexicanos
lejos de la greda azul,
lejos de las rancheras,
muy solos

Your hands
familiar and foreign,
always
your hands
on my lips,
like word-crossings
silences amid the jewels of heaven.

I repeated your name
and the names of the yellow flowers,
tiny wild blossoms.
I also told you
that I loved you
like the one who loves childhood dwellings
where first words reside.

Suddenly,
dimmed before the beauty
we saw them
beyond the abyss.
The men of the vineyards were
somber and downcast,
their skin, clouded
and their hearts imploring;
they were men from a foreign land.

Mejicanos, gathering grapes
in borrowed frontiers.

They didn't see the yellow flowers
or feel the colors of love.
The Mexican men were
far from the blue clay soil,
far from the ranches,

inclinados
pequeñas estatuas.

Mi mirada ya no se detuvo
en una efímera belleza.
Se acercó a ellos,
los supo como los hombres
acusados,
los hombres castigados
por la piel oscura.

Yo me acerqué
a ellos
y les regalé mi corazón,
no les ofrecí flores amarillas,.
Hablé en español
y por un segundo,
no fueron estatuas
sólo hombres.

Tú boca sobre la mía
el amarillo sobre el valle de Napa
donde el general Vallejo nos tricionó
donde los gringoes nos aniquilaron el corazón.
California clara y oscura
tierra de vinos fermentados
y dije:
¡viva México! ¡viva! ¡viva!
y el prado fue rojo calipso turquesa
y las flores amarillas
se desvanecieron
ante la verdadera historia,
y los hombres se llenaron de amapolas
y magueys.

isolated
bent over like
tiny statues.

My gaze no longer lingered
on the ephemeral beauty.
It met them,
and identified their solitude with ours.
It recognized them as men
accused,
men punished for
their dark skin.

I approached
them
and offered them my heart,
not the yellow flowers.
I spoke in Spanish
and for a second
they were not statues
just men.

Your mouth on mine
yellow sprawled over the Napa Valley
where General Vallejo betrayed us
where the gringo annihilated our heart.
Clear and shadowy California,
land of fermented wines
and I said:
Long live Mexico! *Viva! Viva!*
the meadow was a turkish calypso red
and the yellow flowers
faded
before the true story
and the men overflowed with poppies
and magueys.

Una Disculpa

Exijo una disculpa.
Me oyen todos ustedes:
yo, ciudadana de los
ríos de sur;
yo, mujer emigrante involuntaria,
exijo una disculpa
al presidente de los Estados unidos,
ahora y antes
a los secretarios de Estado,
a los agentes de la CIA,
a los soldados,
a la policía secreta de América del Norte,
a los maestros de Georgia que me escupieron el
primer día de clases
y se mofaron de mi estatura y de mi lengua
de mi religión,
aquellos que me llamaron "judía sucia."

Exijo una disculpa.
Desde el *New York Times* hasta
los periódicos de provincia del sur
guardan el solapado silencio
para aparentar los tenues oídos de la
democracia.

Yo exijo una disculpa
porque me robaron a mi país,
el de caracoles y de peces,
el de los moluscos.
Toda mi infancia, saboteada
porque me dejaron para siempre sin patria;
porque tuve que dejar solos a mis muertos

An Apology

I demand an apology.
You hear me, all of you:
I, a citizen of the
Southern rivers;
I, an involuntary woman immigrant,
I demand an apology
from the current and previous
President of the United States,
from the Secretaries of State,
from the CIA agents,
from the soldiers,
from the secret police of North America,
from the Georgia teachers who spit on me
the first day of class
and jeered at my height and my language,
at my religion,
those who called me a "dirty Jew."

I demand an apology.
From the *New York Times* down to the
smallest local papers
of the South, a decorous silence is observed
to soothe the delicate ears of
the democracy.

I demand an apology
because they stole my country from me,
my land of shells and fishes,
my haven of mollusks.
My entire childhood sabotaged
because they left me without a country forever;
because I had to leave my dead all by themselves

y a mis vivos;
porque no pude estar con mis primos.

Ellos se quedaron atrás aguardando cartas.
Yo viajé aguardando cartas
y aún hoy aguardo cartas.
Exijo una disculpa
porque tuve que abandonar mi casa y mis muñecas.
Tuve que viajar como inconclusa,
fugitiva de los territorios prestados.

Exijo una disculpa porque aún no he
cesado de explicarle a todos mis orígenes,
el color de mi pelo, la forma de mi cara,
          el ritmo de mi acento.

Exijo una disculpa porque no puedo hablar
          en español;
porque tuve que aprender otro idioma,
otra forma de hacer matemáticas y el amor.

Exijo una disculpa porque siempre
tengo que explicar mi emigración,
mi raza, mi clase,
el patio de mi casa.

Estoy aquí
porque esta América del Norte
hizo su cositas en
Guatemala, en la República Dominicana,
en Chile, en Costa Rica,
en Cuba,
en todo ese mapa de la esperanza
que es mi América.

and my living, too;
because I didn't get to be with my cousins.

They stayed behind, waiting for letters.
I traveled on, waiting for letters
and today I am still waiting to hear.
I demand an apology
because I had to leave my home and my dolls behind.
I had to leave, an incomplete
fugitive from a borrowed land.

I demand an apology because I still
haven't finished explaining my origins to everyone,
the color of my hair, the shape of my face,
            the rhythm of my accent.

I demand an apology because I cannot speak
            in Spanish;
because I had to learn another language
another way of doing math and making love.

I demand an apology because I always
have to explain why I left,
explain my race, my class,
the patio of my house.

I am here
because this North American country
did its little thing in
Guatemala, in the Dominican Republic,
in Chile, in Costa Rica,
in Cuba,
across the entire map of hope
that is my America.

Exijo una disculpa
por pequeña que sea,
pero entiéndanme bien:
yo perdí lo que fui.

Yo no soy
ni seré.
Todo lo que tenía
se desvaneció como los humos
como las neblinas,
y aquí estoy cada día,
en un tatuaje de memoria,
frágil y sola.

I demand an apology
however small it may be,
but listen closely now:
I lost what I was.
I no longer am
nor will be.
All that I had
faded away like smoke
like mist,
and here I am each day,
marked by the scars of memory,
fragile and alone.

This poem was translated by Mary G. Berg.

Reneé Eppelbaum

Como en un vacío circular
silencioso
sola ha quedado
la Plaza de Mayo
sin ti,
viajera infinita
compañera de los muertos
y de los vivos.

Descansarás en paz
Reneé Eppelbaum
en las puertas de un cielo
imaginario
¿vendrá algún ángel
para aliviar tu vuelo?

Sola ha quedado
la Plaza de Mayo
sin tus pasos lentos y cautelosos
sin tus ojos acostumbrados
a dialogar con la muerte.

Dicen que te has muerto, Reneé,
pero hoy he salido a buscarte
entre los jacarandas,
entre la sombra de todas las ausencias.

Y tu voz me ha cantado
como un aire de la noche
y de pronto
has estado entre las hojas muertas
y tu memoria se ha vuelto
en un don
lleno de claridades
y tus manos
anillo

Reneé Eppelbaum

As in a circular
silent
hollow space,
the Plaza de Mayo
has become lonely without you,
infinite traveler,
companion of the dead
and the living.

You will rest in peace,
Reneé Eppelbaum,
at the gates of an
imaginary heaven.
Will some angel come
to relieve your flight?

The Plaza de Mayo
has become lonely
without your deliberate and cautious steps,
without your eyes accustomed
to speaking with death.

They say that you have died, Reneé,
but today I have gone out to look for you
among the jacarandas,
among the shadows of all the absences.

And your voice has sung to me
like an evening breeze
and suddenly
you have been among the dead leaves
and your memory has returned
with a touch of grace
filled with clarity
and your hands
ring

alianzas
en esta plaza que es
tuya
que te nombra
estás aquí
Reneé visible
circular
danzarina.

Dicen que te has muerto, Reneé,
pero aquí he venido a buscarte
donde alguien rozó mi hombro
y encontró mis manos.

alliances
in this plaza that is
yours,
that names you,
you are here, Reneé,
visible,
circular,
dancing.

They say that you have died, Reneé,
but I have come to look for you here
where someone rubbed my shoulder
and found my hands.

Circles of Madness

❧⊙❧

Círculos de locura

Translated by
Celeste Kostopulos-Cooperman

Winner, 1993 ALTA Prize for Translation

Entonces le pidió
que le guardara sus ojos
en el delantal de percal,
y el otro
le pidió que le guardara
sus manos
en su cintura de hilos,
y la otra le pidió
que enterrara sus piernas
en el jardín de las amapolas
entonces se acercaron todas las madres
entonces se abrieron todos los delantales
como un enorme ataúd
con los sonidos del cielo
entonces sólo quedaron los retratos
de los ojos mancos.

Then he asked her
to keep his eyes
in her apron of percale
and the other
asked her to keep
his hands
on her linen waist
and yet another asked her
to bury her legs
in the garden of the butterflies
then all the mothers approached
then all the aprons opened
like an enormous coffin
with sounds coming from the sky
then all that remained were the pictures
of the maimed eyes.

Cuando encendida la luz de la noche,
y el tiempo es una manta de agua viva,
y el cielo otro silencio aún más silencioso,
cuando las paredes retratan las trizaduras de la mala hora
y todas se duermen en las criptas del insomnio
entonces saco mi fotografía
hago el amor con ella,
la desvisto,
la bailo,
la oigo,
acariciándola,
amándola muy así como en un aire muy dulce,
entonces,
le hablo,
le digo: que bueno que has regresado de los infiernos,
hace tanto tiempo
que no nos vemos;
tanto tiempo sin verte
y la coloco junto
a mi pecho,
me pongo a bailar
con mi muerto
y me pongo a soñar con
mi foto.

When the evening light burns
and time is a blanket of living water,
and the sky another silence even more silent,
when the walls depict the shredded fragments of the evil hour
and everyone falls asleep in the crypts of insomnia
then I take out my photograph
I make love to it,
I undress it,
I dance with it,
I hear it,
caressing it,
and loving it much like a spring of fresh water,
then
I talk to it,
and say: how wonderful that you have returned from hell,
it has been a long time
since we have seen each other;
so much time without seeing you
and I place it close
to my chest,
and I begin to dance
with my dead one
and I begin to dream with
my photo.

¿Ha visto a mi hijo? me
preguntó
tenía una cicatriz alumbradora
en las sienes
tenía los labios de rosa
¿Lo ha visto?
me preguntó
¿O tal vez ha visto
mientras alguien enloquecido
hacía estallar su piel en dolores?
¿Ha visto a mi hijo? me
preguntó
aunque sea por un instante,
¿ha visto a mi hijo?
me dijo
¿Ha visto a mi
hijo?
me volvió a preguntar.

Have you seen my son?
she asked me.
He had a shining scar
on his temple
and rose-colored lips
Have you seen him?
she asked me.
Or did you perhaps witness
some demented person
making his skin explode in piercing pain?
Have you see my son?
she asked me.
Even if only for an instant,
have you seen my son?
she said.
Have you seen
my son?
she continued to ask.

Y a veces me acerco en las puntillas del insomnio mismo,
me detengo
para tocar sus labios
y decirle cosas en secreto
nada demasiado secreto
tan sólo lo que no se le podía decir
mientras lo venían a buscar
mientras lo desnudaban para golpearlo
y dejarlo como una herida en las habitaciones
nebulosas
entonces
yo me acerco
a la orilla misma
de sus labios
que parecen
dos entradas de mar
dos ausencias
que se pueblan de mis palabras
que se estrellan
contra una fotografía
incrustada
en mi alma
como un talismán de mis dolencias.

And sometimes I approach the borders of insomnia
on tiptoe,
I stop
to touch his lips
and to tell him things in secret
nothing too secret
only things that could not be said to him
when they came looking for him
while they undressed him to beat him
and abandon him
like a wounded animal
in the nebulous rooms
then
I approach
the very shore
of his lips
that seem like
two estuaries
two absences
that are filled with my words
that crash
against a photograph
encrusted
in my soul
like a talisman of my sorrows.

Mira,
estas son las fotografías
de mis hijos;
aquí tiene un brazo
no sé si será de mi hijo
pero pienso que tal vez sí
que éste es su brazito de almíbar.
Mira aquí están sus piernas,
cortadas, sajadas
rasgadas
pero son sus piernas
o tal vez las piernas de otro.
No temas.
Son sólo las fotos.
Dicen que es una forma de identificación
y que a lo mejor si te las
muestran
tú misma me ayudarás a encontrarlo.
Mira estas fotografías
regístralas en los álbumes de la vida.

Look,
these are the photographs
of my children;
this one here has an arm
I don't know if it's my son's,
but I think it might be
that this is his sweet little arm.
Look, here are his legs,
severed, cut
and torn
but they are his legs
or perhaps the legs of another.
Don't be afraid.
They are only photographs.
They say it is a form of identification
and if at best they show them
to you
you will be able to help me find him.
Look at these photographs
and record them in the albums of life.

Aquí están nuestros álbumes
éstas son las fotografías
de los rostros
acérquese, no tenga
miedo
¿es verdad que son muy jóvenes? es mi hija,
mire ésta
Andrea y ésta
es mi hija Paola
somos las madres de los
desaparecidos.
Coleccionamos
sus rostros
en estas fotografías
muchas veces hablamos con ellos,
y nos preguntamos:
¿quién acariciará
el pelo de la Graciela?
¿qué habrán hecho con el cuerpecito
de Andrés?
Fíjese que tenían nombres,
les gustaba leer
eran muy jóvenes
ninguno de ellos alcanzó a celebrar
sus dieciocho años,
aquí están sus fotografías,
estos inmensos álbumes
acérquese,
ayúdeme
a lo mejor usted
lo ha visto
y cuando se vaya al extranjero
lleve una de estas fotografías.

Here are our albums,
these are the photographs
of their faces.
Come closer, do not be
afraid.
Isn't it true they're very young? She is my daughter.
Look at this one.
She is Andrea and this
is my daughter Paola.
We are the mothers of the
disappeared.
We collect
their faces
in these photographs
and we often talk with them
and ask ourselves:
Who will caress
Graciela's hair?
What have they done with Andres'
little body?
Notice that they had names,
they liked to read,
they were very young.
None of them ever got to celebrate
their eighteenth birthday.
Here are their photographs,
these immense albums.
Come close,
help me.
Maybe you
have seen him,
and when you travel
take one of these photographs with you.

Cuando me enseñó su fotografía
me dijo
ésta es mi hija
aún no llega a casa
hace diez años que no llega
pero ésta es su fotografía
¿Es muy linda no es cierto?
es una estudiante de filosofía
y aquí está cuando tenía
catorce años
e hizo su primera
comunión
almidonada, sagrada.
Ésta es mi hija
es tan bella
todos los días converso con ella
ya nunca llega tarde a casa, yo por eso la reprocho
mucho menos
pero la quiero tantísimo
ésta es mi hija
todas las noches me despido de ella
la beso
y me cuesta no llorar
aunque sé que no llegará
tarde a casa
porque tú sabes, hace años que
no regresa a casa
yo quiero mucho a esta foto
la miro todos los días
me parece ayer cuando
era un angelito de plumas en mis manos
y aquí está toda hecha una dama
una estudiante de filosofía

When she showed me her photograph
she said,
This is my daughter.
She still hasn't come home.
She hasn't come home in ten years.
But this is her photograph.
Isn't it true that she is very pretty?
She is a philosophy student
and here she is when she was
fourteen years old
and had her first
communion,
starched, sacred.
This is my daughter.
She is so pretty.
I talk to her every day.
She no longer comes home late, and this is why I reproach her
much less.
But I love her so much.
This is my daughter.
Every night I say goodbye to her.
I kiss her
and it's hard for me not to cry
even though I know she will not come
home late
because as you know, she has not come
home for years.
I love this photo very much.
I look at it every day.
It seems that only yesterday
she was a little feathered angel in my arms
and here she looks like a young lady,
a philosophy student,

una desaparecida
pero ¿no es cierto que es tan linda,
que tiene un rostro de angel.
que parece que estuviera viva?

another disappeared.
But isn't it true that she is so pretty,
that she has an angel's face,
that it seems as if she were alive?

I.
Como un ave migratoria, ella se deplaza entre los muebles
vendados, como si toda la habitación fuera un solo precipicio que
la golpea, que la desdibuja y entre las tinieblas de los
videntes, ella se pregunta sobre la felicidad de aquella sagrada,
casi imaginaria familia.

II.
Ilumina los adioses de la pequeña Lila,
recuerda el beso de Claudito,
recuerda los pies, el agua, el ruido de los tiernos
ríos, en sus palmas,
las piedras en los rincones de cada bolsillo amado
entonces enciende las lámparas del amor
y pareciera que se desnudara en un lienzo de cantares
y pareciera que ellos lloraran.

III.
De sus bocas salen
pájaros,
el nombre de los hijos
y de los hijos
de las otras
y las otras
también dicen el nombre de las otras y otros hijos de otras,
se buscan
se humedecen
abandonadas se recogen,
son las Madres de la Plaza de Mayo.

I.
Like a migratory bird, she unfurls herself among the draped
furniture, as if the entire room were a dangerous edge that
erases her, that draws her faded outline, and in the
blindness of those who see, she asks herself about the happiness
of that sacred,
almost imaginary family.

II.
She illuminates the good-byes of little Lila,
she remembers Claudito's kiss,
she remembers the feet, the water, the sound of the tender
river, and in her palms
the stones from the corners of each beloved pocket.
Then she turns on the night lights
and it seems as if she were undressing in a canvas of songs
and it seems as if they were crying.

III.
Flying from their mouths
like birds
the names of the children
and of the children
of the others,
and the others
also repeat the names of the others
and of other children of others.
They look for each other.
They cry.
Abandoned, they gather together,
the Mothers of the Plaza de Mayo.

Cartas de agua

Enmudecida repleta de ternura,
lee las cartas de agua,
y las voces de los idos
florecen en su piel de durezas.
Parece que está tocando ternuras,
que escucha las palabras de los idos, ya ajenos
enmudecida,
lee y relee, revisa, resalta
las cartas de agua,
y la risa de los desaparecidos
la vigila la puebla de pájaros.

Panuelos

Los pañuelos que atan, que se desatan, enloquecidos silban, besan, gimen. Dénme un pañuelo contra la injusticia, dénme una mano para extenderme, para hacerme un solo quejido cubriéndote. Dénme un pañuelo contra la injusticia, para ser el blanco retazo de una ausencia, para no ser una extranjera de huesos mancos. Yo quiero un pañuelo contra la injusticia, para cubrirte, para danzarte en los lienzos alados de la paz, para llenarte de caricias y hacerte soñar en una memoria de tu cuerpo así muy junto al mío, como si fuéramos los natalicios de los ríos.

Misty Letters

Speechless and full of tenderness,
she reads the misty letters,
and the voices of the departed
flourish within her hardened skin.
It looks like she is playing tender tunes,
like she is listening to the words of the departed,
now distant, voiceless.
She reads and rereads, examines and lets go
the misty letters
and the laughter of the disappeared
watches over her, crowning her with birds.

Kerchiefs

The kerchiefs that they tie, that are untied, madly whistle, kiss and moan.
Give me a kerchief against injustice, give me a hand to stretch out so I may
become a solitary lament that covers you. Give me a kerchief against injus-
tice, so that I may be a white remnant of an absence, so that I will not be a
foreigner of maimed bones. I want a kerchief against injustice so I can
cover you, dance with you on the winged banners of peace, fill you up
with caresses, and make you dream about a memory of your body very
close to mine, as if we were two joining fountainheads.

¿Cuántas veces yo converso con mis muertos
y sus manos, son una textura hundida, y les pregunto cosas
y sus rostros son una memoria de llagas, y la noche
amenazándonos en su caída intempestuosa, pero yo converso con
mis muertos que a lo mejor son tuyos, y los cubro, los empapo
de mi sentir callado y de mis ojos parecidos a los alambres de la
sombra. Siempre me despido de ese cuerpo, de esos ojos que me parecen
un río
de silencio.
Y así aprendo a decirles cosas,
a prometerles un jardín floreciente, florido,
una historia, un nacimiento, una promesa,
y es tan increíble como yo amo a este muerto, que no es mi
muerto,
que tampoco es un cadáver. Es un salto de agua, un diálogo,
una costa para cruzar.

How many times do I talk with my dead?
And their hands are rough and wrinkled, and I ask them
things and their faces are a memory of sorrows, and the night
threatens us in its tempestuous fall, but I talk with
my dead which perhaps are yours, and I cover them, saturate
them with my silent sorrow and with my tear-drenched eyes.
I always bid farewell to that body,
to those eyes that seem like a river
of silence.
And this is how I learn to tell them things,
to promise them a blossoming, flowery garden,
a history, a beginning, a promise,
and it is so incredible how I love this dead one, who is not mine,
who is not a cadaver either, but a waterfall, a dialogue,
a shore to be crossed.

Con paciencia ellas los nombran, como si se tratara de leyendas.
Pero son los hijos, y nadie asiste a las ceremonias y nadie se
asoma por las antesalas de los idos.

Los jacarandás, esparciendo decires, hechizándonos con el olor
intempestuoso de sus fragancias, lejanas como las fotografías de las memorias dislocadas. Los jacarandás, haciendo alianzas con los enamorados o sombra con los ancianos transeúntes. Los jacarandás, cubriendo ataúdes y presagios, acercándome al retrato de mi hija Lila, en una ciudad invisible sin mar. Cóncava ausencia dolida en los dolidos sueños.

The patiently name them, as if dealing with legends.
But they are their children and no one attends the ceremonies
and no one looks out of the antechambers of the departed.

The jacarandás, spreading their scent, charming us with the tempestuous
odor of their fragrance, distant like photographs of dislocated memories.
The jacarandás, making alliances with the lovers or offering shade to the
old passers-by. The jacarandás, covering coffins and omens, drawing me
toward the portrait of my daughter Lila in an invisible city without a
seashore. A concave and painful absence locked within my painful dreams.

Desfiles

Bajo sus ojos lleva las cicatrices de la ausencia y su caminar es
un juego de dados tambaleándose, fracturándose en los indicios
del miedo. Ella desfila, se alarga, y el dolor la extiende,
haciéndola cada vez más una inmensa pirámide de soles y
estiércoles. Dice que busca a sus vivos o a sus muertos. Y ella
desfila, contornea, y su pañuelo es un solo delirio como las
señales de la muerte.
En la noche todo es ausencia y el día es una invención maldita.
No hay duelo para la buscadora.

Y el silencio de los cuerpos que anidan la acompaña
y la noche misma es un estrepitoso silencio dislocado, alado, es
cóncavo entre sus pasos de niebla.

Processions

Beneath her eyes she carries the scars of absence, and her gait
is like a tottering game of dice rupturing in the vestiges
of fear. She marches, she stretches, and her grief expands,
increasingly transforming her into an immense pyramid of sunflowers
and dung. She says that she is looking for either her living or her dead.
And she marches and goes round, and her kerchief is a singular delirium,
like the signs of death.
At night all is absence, and the day is an evil invention.
There is no mourning for the seeker.

And the silence of the nested bodies accompanies her,
and night itself is a deafening, dislocated, winged silence,
a concave surface beneath her nebulous steps.

Y entonces las iluminadas hicieron altares. Una trajo un peine de nácar, otra un brillo de arena, una pala con estrellas. Entonces, una esperó hasta la médula misma de la oscuridad oscurísima, y comenzó a enterrar las prendas, los enormes suéteres tejidos a palillo, y la lana se tiñó de nácar, y el viento mismo la cubrió con la lana de estrellas. Entonces descansaron, dejaron de rondar enloquecidas, y alguien prendió unas velas para acompañar a los vivos.

Vacíos para siempre han quedado
los armarios, y ella conversa en la orilla de una cama
que se escurre, flota, y es un oficio de tinieblas,
donde el cuerpo ido deja una huella que corroe
y ella, arqueada, palpa las camisas
y palpa las fotografías
de los nobles días de la vida.
Entonces se pone
a cantar
a pesar de las densas neblinas,
entonces se pone a cantar.

And then the visionaries made altars. One brought a mother-of-pearl comb, another a shining grain of sand, a shovel full of stars. Then one waited until the very heart of darkness and began to bury the tokens and the enormous hand-knitted sweaters, their wool stained like mother-of-pearl, and the wind covered her with its blanket of stars. Then they rested, they stopped hovering like madwomen, and someone lighted candles to accompany the living.

The closets have remained empty forever,
and she converses at the edge of a bed
that glides, floats, and is a ritual of darkness
where the absent body leaves an impression that corrodes,
and she, crouching, caresses the shirts,
and caresses the photographs
of the noble days of life.
And then she begins
to sing,
in spite of the dense mist,
then she begins to sing.

Y entonces se lanzaban en el aire denso, alguien las
quemaba, sajándolas, rapándolas,
y parecían unas personas de plumas, jamás altivaś, arrastrándose
para que la muerte alada no se las llevase, y danzaban con un
rito parecido a los delirios.

Entonces llevaban pañuelos blancos, de la misma forma en que
se lleva un amor.

La vieron sujetar a su mismísima cintura y el roce de sus manos alargaba
sus formas dislocadas. Parecía un espejo de agua, solísima, contemplando,
y no sabían si hacer los bailes del duelo o de la vida. Y ella no sabía si era
una danzante de agua o una estremecida madre sujetándose el desgarro de
esos nacimientos, o al hijo que mecía muerto en sus sueños—memoria—en
su país de humo.

And then they were hurled into the dense air, someone was
burning them, cutting them, shaving them,
and they seemed like feathered beings, never lofty,
crawling, so that winged death would not carry them off
and they danced in a ceremonial delirium.

Then they wore white kerchiefs, the same way
love is worn.

They saw her grasp her own waist, and the friction from her hands length-
ened her dislocated form. She seemed like a looking-glass of water, contem-
plating, all alone, and they didn't know whether to have a dance of grief or
of life. And she didn't know whether she was a water dancer or a trembling
mother, holding on to the laceration of those births or to the son she
rocked dead in her dreams—a memory—in her land of smoke.

La niebla iracunda precisa asomándose por las hendiduras del jardín, a lo lejos alguien canta una memoria de lilas, alguien se pregunta por los pétalos del ensueño. Alguien dice, con una voz de mujer extraviada, que la loca plantaba lilas en el medio del musgo habitado, y entre los jardines, se asoman lo niños muertos porque no quieren estar muertos, porque aún quieren vestirse y ser lilas, y las locas ellas, ellas las locas, matutinas, como si fueran espejos de clarividencias-claroscuras, se asoman, y los acechan tras los rosales, debajo de las amapolas, porque ¿quién no tiene un niño detrás de un manojo de esperanzas? ¿Quién no ha visto a un niño detrás de la anchura de los árboles?

The irascible distinct mist peeks through the crevices of the garden. In the distance someone sings a memory of lillies, and someone else asks for the petals of a daydream. Someone with a deranged woman's voice says the madwoman would plant lilies in the middle of spreading moss, and that the dead children appear in the gardens because they don't want to be dead, because they still want to dress up and be lillies, and the mad-women, the matutinal madwomen, appear like mirrors of clairvoyant chiaroscuros, and they watch them from behind the rose bushes and from beneath the poppies because who doesn't have a child behind a handful of hope? Who has not seen a child hiding behind a tree trunk?

Y estaban,
en los nichos o en las criptas de lo más mudo,
cada una de ellas insistía en precisar miradas,
un hombre, sujetando otra mano, ella con pan en los brazos,
dibujaban el cielo con la memoria,
y armaban los rostros con los pedazos perdidos
como quien se pone a tejer las cavidades, las
quebraduras, un eclipse de vidrios cortados, requebrados una
y otra vez,
y ellas tranquilas, como caracoles, arrastrándose, recostándose,
perdiéndose en el deseo
querían
que aparecieran
con vida, con luz, con vida viva
¿cómo hacer de aquellos trozos de manos solitarias insondables,
un ser, una iluminación de palabras,
una infancia germinando en las trincheras?
Entonces, ellas sólo dibujan a un cuerpo sobre el pavimento,
y lo desnudan en los nudos de tiza, blanca,
y del pavimento mismo nacen ruidos, quejidos que nadie sabe, que
nadie quiere, que nadie pregunta.
¿Y, cómo hablar de los muertos?

And they were
in the recesses or the crypts of the most silent,
each one of them insisting on specifying images,
a man, holding another hand, a woman with bread in her arms,
they drew the sky with their memories
and formed faces out of missing pieces
like someone who begins weaving holes,
fractures, an eclipse of cut glass broken over
and over again,
and peaceful as snails, creeping, reclining and
losing themselves in desire,
they wanted
them to appear
with life, with light, with vivid life.
How can
a being, an illumination of words,
a childhood sprouting in the ditches
be made from those fragments of solitary, unreachable hands?
So they only draw the outline of a body on the pavement,
they lay it bare in lumps of white chalk,
and from the pavement arise noises and laments that
no one knows, that no one wants, that no one questions.
For how do you talk about the dead?

Una mujer aguarda a sus muertos, en un comedor
insensato. Aulla esos nombres como los dados de la muerte; se
resfriega los ojos y pide verlos mejor,
decirles cosas como el color del cielo en los parques,
o el porqué de las lluvias en una mirada.
Una mujer habla de la muerte como si fuera una vagabunda en
rotaciones ancladas.
Una mujer conversa con la muerte en
un comedor de sillas mancas, de
tenedores carmesíes, un cuchillo
solitario
desfila en la penumbra
Una mujer aguarda a sus muertos.

A woman waits for her dead in a useless
dining room. She howls those names
like the dice of death; she clears her eyes
and asks to see them better,
to tell them things like the color of the sky
in the parks,
or the reason for her tear-drenched look.
A woman talks about death as if it were a vagabond
moving in a tethered circle.
A woman converses with death in
a dining room of maimed chairs,
scarlet-colored forks, and a
solitary knife
marching in the semi-darkness.
A woman waits for her dead.

Como la suavidad de los comienzos

I.
Entonces el despertar del alba intrépida
y ahí están, somos
fotografías inmóviles
sobre unas llagas movedizas.
Ahí están las fotos estáticas, acechándola,
mirándola mientras obstinada sacude los muebles y entran por los
umbrales los vientos de los desaparecidos.

II.
Se dirige a los armarios,
a las camas,
asea
una casa que gime
donde nadie llega ni regresa, ni golpea
tan sólo los vientos de los desaparecidos.

III.
Ella igual busca,
apaga la luz, el hueso de la memoria
no duerme,
los saluda,
sólo fotos, estampas anonadadas.
Y los vientos de los desaparecidos
la golpean.

As Gentle as Beginnings

I.
The intrepid dawn awakens
and here they are, we are
motionless photographs
on shifting sorrows.
Here are the still photos, watching her,
looking at her as she obstinately dusts the furniture
and the spirits of the disappeared come through the door.

II.
She goes to the closets,
to the beds,
she cleans
a house that moans,
where no one arrives, returns, or knocks,
except for the spirits of the disappeared.

III.
She also searches,
turns off the light, and in the depths of memory
does not sleep.
She greets them,
only photos, annihilated prints,
and the spirits of the disappeared
wound her.

De puntillas se alzaban, ebrias en su fatalidad, y cada pisada dejaba las huellas de un insomnio. Extrañamente, sus pañuelos parecían ser alas o el sonido de la lluvia, transmutado en neblinas, y así iban las brujas de la verdad, deslizándose, inventando clarividencias ingénuas. Parecían ser una sola banda de aves, victimarias y magas. Ahí estaban detenidas, movedizas, extrañas forasteras. Y la plaza era una fiesta iluminada.

Comienzan a moverse, lentas, lentísimas. Alguien las suspende desde la altura misma de los pies. Parecen danzar y trenzarse hacia la deriva. Míralas cómo se estremecen para construir rondas y bailan cada vez más afiebradas, poseídas, en la raíz misma de una locura enfermiza. Bailan alrededor de los muertos, exigen espacios, piden saber, y bailan, y bailan como si fuera este baile el último round del alma.

They arose on tiptoe, intoxicated in their doom, and each footstep left behind traces of insomnia. Strangely, their kerchiefs seemed like wings or like the sound of falling rain transmuted into mist, and this is how the witches of truth went about, slipping away and inventing ingenuous visions. They seemed like a solitary flock of birds, assassins, and witches. There they were, timid, unsteady, and strange outsiders. And the plaza was a feast of lights.

They begin to move slowly, sluggishly, as if someone were suspending them from high above. They seem to dance and to swagger off course. Look at them and how they quiver to form circles and each time they dance more feverishy, possessed, near the very root of a sickly madness. They dance around the dead, they demand space, they demand to know, and they dance, and they dance as if this dance were the last round of their souls.

I.
Hermana amada,
mujer de cicatrizes y solsticios
amiga de los pordioseros
eterna compañera de los torturados
ven, ayúdame en la amanecida.
Déjame poner un sueño en tus faldas
que lavaron el dolor agrio, inundado, de los despellejados.

II.
Déjame morirme
en tus brazos de sol y sangre que se
deshacen para volver a llenarse
de veranos fresas, pieles alegres del Sur.

III.
Amiga mía,
hermana,
amada danzarina de las fuentes,
de los cuerpos que acechan la extensión del amor,
déjame ser palabra en tu ausencia.

IV.
Amada, mientras alzas tus manos
y tus palmas son los senderos,
los ríos, las historias de luces y luciérnagas
madre amada
compañera de planetas, duelos y nacimientos
verde, verdosa dama
déjame ser
tu hija.

I.
Beloved sister,
woman of scars and solstices
friend of beggars
eternal companion of the tortured
come, help me at the break of dawn.
In your skirts that washed the bitter,
inundated grief of the despoiled,
let me place a dream.

II.
Let me die
in your arms of sunlight and blood that
dissolve to fill up again
with summer strawberries and bright southern hides.

III.
My friend,
sister
beloved dancer of the fountains
and of the bodies that wait for love's embrace,
let me be the word in your absence.

IV.
Beloved, as you raise your hands
and your palms become the trails,
the rivers, the stories of light and fireflies,
beloved mother,
companion of planets, tribulations and births,
green, greenish lady
let me be
your daughter.

Maga vidente,
violada cada tres segundos,
déjame ponerte una colcha de sueños,
déjame hacer con el cuerpo
una playa, un girasol, los vientos de la delicia
porque en tus manos anidan
los sin puertas,
los que ocupan el espacio
de las aceras agrietadas,
porque en tu palabra,
aparecen los muertos-vivos
jamás igualados,
jamás enterrados,
los muertos,
que ocupan tus llagas en las miradas,
los muertos, que cabalgan en tus alientos,
y te besan tus pechos con tanta sed y sangre.
Madre amada,
eres un faro con ritmo de gaviota
una ruta secreta con tus anhelos bordados
con nombres de vivos y muertos,
muertos y vivos,
déjame llorar en tus tinieblas,
bañarme en la luz de la victoria silenciosa.

Luminous sage,
desecrated every three seconds,
let me cover you with a blanket of dreams,
let me make your body
a seashore, a sunflower, winds of delight
because in your hands live
the homeless,
those that occupy the space
of the cracked sidewalks,
because in your word
appear the living dead,
never equaled,
never buried,
the dead,
that live in your looks of pain,
the dead,
that ride in your breaths
and kiss your breasts with so much thirst and blood.
Beloved mother,
you are a beacon with a seagull's rhythm,
a secret route with your desires embroidered
with the names of the living and the dead,
the dead and the living,
let me cry in your darkness,
and bathe in the light of silent victory.

Memorial

La memoria como un trozo de lienzo impreciso y bello
acumulando los rescoldos de la ira,
las bellezas de una ternura amplia y
dibujada
en la raíz misma de una espada de fe se extiende para
ser una mesa donde
cada uno escribe lo que quiere
o no quiere recordar:
una espalda de madera lisa para inventar los
mapas de las cosas queridas,
la memoria volando en el revés mismo del cielo
oscura y luminosa,
doblada y siempre
haciéndose a sí misma
como un collar de palabras
entre las piedras cautivadas,
las que nada pueden decir.

Memorial

Memory, like a piece of beautiful and imprecise canvas
accumulating the embers of wrath,
the beauties of an expansive tenderness that is
stretched
to the very base of a sword of faith which expands
to become a table where
everyone writes what he wants
or does not want to remember:
a blade of smooth wood where we can invent
maps to our most cherished possessions,
memory flying opposite the sky,
dark and luminous,
folded and always
transforming itself
into a necklace of words
strung between the captive stones
that cannot say anything.

Las flores amarillas
destapadas reposando sobre las yerbas sedosas
parecen ser las faldas que el viento levanta y trepa
y soplan en una luz ténue de gracias secretas
y adivinan los sueños de los desvalidos
espectadores
de las mujeres solísimas
que buscan una flor amarilla de la amanecida
en sus contornos
que buscan una ráfaga de amarillos
para las tumbas
sin nombre.

The yellow flowers
uncovered and resting on the silken grass
seem like skirts that the wind lifts and mounts
and they blow in a tenuous light of secret graces,
foretelling the dreams of the unprotected
spectators,
of the very lonely women
who watch from their outposts
for a yellow flower of dawn,
who look for a gust of yellow blossoms
for the tombs
of the nameless.

Ella es un soliloquio entre sus pasos, una alquimia de la vida misma, erguida, descalza, altísima en su silencio y en la plenitud de sus inmensas abiertas palmas. Va hacia el río, un abrazo de agua marca sus travesías y en el río ondulado leve, ella alza sus manos, para encontrarlo, hallarlo, decirle en el oído los sonidos del agua y ella se transforma en árbol, porque sus brazos son dos ramas floridas mientras lo busca en el río, y cuando no aparece entonces, ella se acerca al mar, a los inmensos territorios de las costas y al aliento indomable de la deriva.

A veces ya no divisa al río o lo confunde con la plena mar. A veces, regresa descalza en una sola caricia mojada y sueña con las penas, y sueña con ir otra vez veloz al río porque a lo mejor verá sus cabellos castaños, soleados, si no está en el río, a lo mejor, sí, seguro que estará en el mar. Si no estará en el mar, seguro en el cielo de la tierra.

Walking, she is a soliloquy, an alchemy of life itself, erect, barefoot, majestic in her silence and in the plenitude of her immense open palms. She goes to the river; an embrace of water outlines her crossings, and in the light rippling river, she raises her hands to find him, to discover him, and to whisper water sounds in his ear, and she becomes a tree because her arms are two flowery branches while she looks for him, and when he does not appear, she then approaches the sea, the immense territories of the coasts and the dauntless vigor of the surging tide.

Sometimes she no longer sees the river or she confuses it with the whole sea. Sometimes she returns barefoot in a lonely wet caress and dreams about her sorrows, and she dreams about returning quickly to the river because maybe she will see his brown sun-bleached locks of hair, and if he is not in the river, maybe, yes, surely he will be in the sea. If he isn't in the sea, surely he will be in heaven.

Sonidos

Las palabras se desgarraron del sonido.
Emigraron feroces en el comienzo de mi labio.
Cosas extrañas se colaban en mi sed,
flores no fecundadas
hervían en mi paladar
amordazado.
Emigré de mí misma,
quise condenarme en el abecedario de las mudas,
para así no gritar,
así no ahullar,
para así decir sin el decir.
Las palabras desgarraron la oscuridad de mi tiniebla enmudecida.
Quise ser entonces
la palabra misma de la voz,
repetir un nombre.

Sounds

The words broke away from the sound.
They emigrated ferociously to the edge of my lips.
Strange things filtered into my thirst, fruitless
flowers seethed in my
silenced palate.
I emigrated from myself;
I tried to condemn myself to the language of the deaf,
so as not to cry out,
so as not to wail,
so as to tell without telling.
The words tore into the obscurity of my silenced darkness.
Then I tried to be
the spoken word,
so I could repeat a name.

Poema para recitar in los sueños del mar

Y en la noche, los sonidos de la noche ocre y alucinada, destartalada e imprecisa; y en la noche ella busca una memoria, y se llama en voz alta y se acaricia el pelo hasta hacerse una herida, siempre en las manos. Y los sonidos de la noche, la acercan a otras noches y a noches parecidas a las maderas húmedas, parecidas a las casas que aguardan a sus huéspedes para colmarlos de una luz como las estaciones invencibles del sueño.

Poem to be Recited in Dreams of the Sea

At night, in the sounds of an ocher and hallucinatory, confused and imprecise night, she searches for a memory and shouts her name and caresses her hair until a wound appears, always in her hands. And the night sounds draw her closer to other nights, to nights resembling humid wood piles, resembling homes that wait for their guests to adorn them with light like the invincible seasons of dream.

Las madres de los presos políticos
no se endurecen ni llevan en sus
rostros las huellas y trazos del dolor
las mujeres de los presos
políticos llevan el pan de la victoria
cuando se acercan por las rendijas aterradoras del vacío
y cuando reparten pan, maíz, y sol,
la cárcel se llena de pájaros y brazos cantores
las mujeres de los presos políticos
no lloran cuando se despiden
de los maridos condenados a muerte
de los recientemente torturados
ellas cantan un himno parecido
a los diluvios o a los profundos arcoiris
de las delicias
y se van
marchando
y entre sus faldas
germinan niños
y en vez de incendios y lápidas
se repiten como los ríos y la vida
y no son nada de parecidas
a los tacones solapados de
la muerte.

Mothers of political prisoners
do not get hardhearted, nor do they carry in their
faces traces and outlines of pain.
Women of political prioners
carry victory bread
when they approach the terrifying cracks of the void
and when they hand out bread, corn, and sunshine,
the prison fills up with birds and singing arms.
Women of political prisoners
don't cry when they bid farewell
to their spouses condemned to death,
to the recently tortured.
They sing a hymn that resembles
floods or deep rainbows
of delight
and they leave
marching
and between their skirts
sprout children
and instead of fires and gravestones
they repeat themselves like rivers and life
and they don't seem anything
like the furtive heels of
death.

Transparentes,
los cofres de la memoria.
El aire se vuelve hundido
en su frente que arde y clama.
Su vista hinchada es una sola mirada de espanto,
un huracán de ojos detenidos.
Ella saca las cartas
de sus tres muertos
o vivos,
y una voz de música y esencia
y un amanecer de agua los envuelve.
Todo se ancla en el silencio
y ella camina tranquila
errando los cofres,
cerrando el incendio
de sus ojos que palpitan presencias.

Transparent
coffers of memory.
The air becomes deep-set
in her burning and clamoring forehead.
Her swollen glance is a solitary look of fright,
a hurricane of shiftless eyes.
She gets the letters
of her three dead
or live ones,
and a voice of music and fragrance
and a dawn of water surrounds them.
Everything is anchored in silence
and she walks peacefully
missing the coffers,
and putting out the fire
in her eyes that throb with presences.

Y sus labios comenzaban a abrirse muy lentamente como si fueran magas salidas

de un sueño herido y había en ellas el movimiento de pájaros incendiados.

Caminaban confundiéndose con los gestos de los árboles que parecían hijos

meciéndose y era una sola muchedumbre transparente mientras espectadores
y

difuntos huían aterrados. Las sabias magas que parecían sombras aclaradas por

la misma luz que las sujetaba, comenzaron a pedir cosas: una decía "háblame,
háblame," y otra llamaba a un niño perdido.

Todos sus cuerpos se doblaban

y no por el viento

ni por los árboles que las envolvían cada vez más estrechamente cuando

llamaban. Eran mujeres jóvenes con niños en los brazos.

Yo tampoco las pude dejar de pensar

porque parecían huérfanas que me llamaban

y decían

no me dejes

yo no podía no ser algo de ellas, ni dejarlas,

porque sería como dejar

a mi madre

sin sus huesos,

sin hija

dejarlas así, todas abiertas y llenas

de valles oscuros.

Entonces yo también comencé a acercarme,

a pronunciar algo que me mordía desde muy adentro.

Y mientras oía, oíamos el ulular de las sirenas

y mis labios también se convirtieron en pájaros

y mis manos en árboles

y mis palabras

en miles de rostros.

And their lips began to open very slowly as if they were
sages escaping from a wounded dream, and in them was
a movement of burning birds. They walked confusing
themselves with the gestures of the trees that seemed like
children rocking, and it was a single transparent crowd
while spectators and corpses fled in terror. The wise
sages seemed like shadows clarified by the
same light that subdued them, and they began to ask for
things. One said "Talk to me, talk to me,"
the other called out to a lost child.
All their bodies bent
not because of the wind
nor because of the trees that surrounded them more
each time they called. They were
young women with children in their arms.
I also could not stop thinking of them
because they seemed like orphans calling me
and saying:
don't leave me.
I could not refrain from becoming part of them, nor
could I abandon them,
because it would be like leaving
my own mother
without her bones,
without her daughter,
leaving them like this, everyone open and full
of obscure valleys.
Then I also began to approach,
to give voice to something that was eating me away inside.
And while I listened we heard the screeching of sirens
and my lips became birds
and my hands, trees
and my words
thousands of faces.

Zones of Pain

~~~

Translated by Cola Franzen

Prólogo

Las desaparedidas se deslizaron entre los sueños. Me vigilaban, a veces me despertaban acariciándome, más que nada me pedian que no las olivide. Así fueron creciendo estas Zonas del dolor. Ellas, las mujeres enterradas pero siempre vivas fabricaron las urdimbres de mis palabras que en la humildad de la impotencia buscaron claridades y voces.

Las zonas del dolor representan la travesía de las enterradas, como también la travesía de las madres buscadoras. Las zonas del dolor son nuestras, son oscuras, y a veces demasiado olvidadizas. Por ese yo las escribi, porque quise acompañar a mis hermanas muertas.e

Prologue

The disappeared women slipped in among dreams. They would watch me, at times they would wake me up caressing me, more than anything else they would ask me not to forget them. That's how these Zones of Pain kept growing. The women, buried but still alive, wove the fabric of my words that in the humility of helplessness sought for clear places and voices.

The zones of pain represent the wandering of buried women and the wandering of searching mothers. The zones of pain are ours, are dark, and at times too easily slip the mind. For these reasons I wrote them down, because I wish to accompany my dead sisters.

Tras el alba

Tras el alba
envestida de niebla,
le preguntaron
¿por pué llorba?
¿qué a quién buscaba?
—ella sólo les dijo
devuélvanme a mi
hija.

Beyond the Dawn

Beyond the dawn
clothed in fog,
they asked her
why are you weeping?
who are you seeking?
—she only said to them
give me back my
daughter.

Las zonas del dolor

Lasa zonas del dolor, inquietas, desplazadas
amasadas más allá del tiempo siniestro.
Como páramos o selvas calcinadas,
las zonas del dolor,
se asoman adoloridas, retrocediéndose en una charca de artificios
inútiles.

Las zonas del dolor
habitando el festín de los mancos.
Sobre las quebraduras,
el dolor tapiza heridas abiertas.
y entre las llamas de lo que no pudo
ser,
en los errores del azar,
las zonas del dolor
encuentran su litigio.

Adormecen al cuerpo desprendido de su carne,
al cuerpo encendido en sus propias navegaciones,

Las zonas del dolor,
se entristecen, cuando los sobrevivientes
ofrecen regazos para los muertos-malheridos.

Zones of Pain

The zones of pain, restless, scattered
massed beyond the sinister time.
Like barrens or burnt-over forests,
the zones of pain
rise up painfully, fall back into a puddle of useless
ruses.

The zones of pain
inhabit the banquet of the maimed.
Over the burns,
the pain covers open wounds,
and among the flames of what could not
be,
in the errors of chance,
the zones of pain
find their redress.

They put to sleep the body stripped of its flesh,
the body on fire sailing its own course.

The zones of pain
are saddened when survivors
offer solace to the dead-dying.

Zonas del dolor II

El dolor, salvaje y preciso
sin cautela,
estalla sobre la arena del cuerpo,
brilla, acelerado, sobre las huellas
ardientes de mil hogueras.
Alguien juega con la miseria
de este cuerpo postrado,
de esta soledad entre
las piernas
que aullan.

II.
Las venas adiestradas
lentamente se abren,
dejan que la vida atraviese
y las llagas del
alma crecen entre
las tinieblas.

El dolor salvaje y preciso
cruza el umbral de la
duermevela
ahora sueño entre
los delirios.

Zones of Pain II

The pain, savage and exact
without guile,
explores over the sands of the body,
glows, speeded over the burning
traces of a thousand bonfires.
Someone toys with the misery
of this prostrate body,
of this solitude between
the howling
legs.

II.
The obedient veins
open slowly
let the life pass through
and the wounds of the
soul flourish in
the darkness.

The pain savage and exact
crosses the threshold of
half-sleep
now dream amid
the delirium.

La mano

Alguien herida,
transmutada
me toma de la mano,
y entre la sombra
tras los abismos
esa mano asegurándome las
cadencias de
la mía
me regresa al
rastro
de tus yemas que desordenamente
celebraban mi cabello.

II.
Esas manos pertenecen al incierto paraíso
de un ajeno próximo a mi,
que me cuida sujetándome
de la mano,
así, suave, muy suave,
para que nadie nos delate en
ese gesto que cruza orillas
y habita cálido entre las memorias.

III.
En esta instancia
deshabitada,
alguien me toma de la mano
y sus caricias son los sollozos de
mi niño muerto
y sus yemas
el sueño de los
vivos.

The Hand

Someone wounded,
transmuted
takes me by the hand,
and through the shadow
behind the chasms
her hand assures me of
the rhythms
of mine,
brings me back to the
trace
of your fingertips that tousle and
celebrate my hair.

II.
Those hands belong to an uncertain paradise
of a stranger next to me,
who cares for me, holding me
by the hand,
like this, softly, very softly,
so that nobody can catch us in
that gesture that crosses borders
and dwells warm among the memories.

III.
In this emptied
instant,
someone takes me by the hand
and her caresses are the sobs of
my dead son
and her fingertips
the dream of the
living ones.

Lo más increíble

Lo más increíble
eran gente como nosotros
bien educados y finos.
Versados en las ciencias abstractas,
asistían al palco de las sinfonías
al dentista
a las escuelitas privadas
algunos jugaban al golf...

Sí, gente como usted, como yo
padres de familia
abuelos
tíos y compadres.

Pero enloquecieron
se deleitaban en las quemas
de niños y libros,
jugaban a decorar cementerios
compraban muebles de huesos mancos
comían orejitas y testículos.

Se figuraban ser invencibles
ceremoniosos ante el deber
y hablaban de la tortura
con palabras de médicos y carniceros.

The most unbelievable part

The most unbelievable part,
they were people like us
good manners
well-educated and refined.
Versed in abstract sciences,
always took a box for the symphony
made regular trips to the dentist
attended very nice prep schools
some played golf.

Yes, people like you, like me
family men
grandfathers
uncles and godfathers.

But they went crazy
delighted in burning
children and books
played at decorating cemeteries
bought furniture made of broken bones
dined on tender ears and testicles.

Thought they were invincible
meticulous in their duties
and spoke of torture
in the language of surgeons and butchers.

Asesinaron a los jóvenes de mi páis.
y del tuya.
Ya nadie podría creer en Alicia tras los espejos
ya nadie podría pasearse por las avenidas
sin el terror calándose entre los huesos.

Y lo más increíble
era gente
como usted
como yo
sí, gente fina
como nosotros.

They assassinated the young of my country
and of yours.
Now nobody could believe in Alice through the looking glass,
now nobody could stroll along the avenues
without terror bursting through their bones.

And the most unbelievable part
they were people
like you
like me
yes, nice people
just like us.

La Tortura

—Para Rosa Montero y para aquellos que le contaron sus historias

Lentemente, cautelosamente,
ardía mi paladar silenciado
mientras ya desnuda y
tan lejana
conspiraban para atrapar
mis pezones, pequeños alambres de espanto.
Sus manos pequeñas, perdidas de escamas agrias
viajaban por esa lenta agonía, por su oscurecida
claridad entre mis piernas
y ellos, los ociosos verdugos
jadeaban mientras
la sangre de la luna
aullaba en las tablas
de un metal enfermizo,
me limpiaban la frente
para después verter las
desquiciadas palmas de mi historia
y entre el vacío del tiempo
entre los segundos del aire
una electricidad de lanzas y lágrimas
se desprendía como las hojas de un otoño de guerreros desquiciados
las uñas extendidas sobre el suelo en llamas y menses,
los dientes machacados por picanas y escupos traicioneros,
se desligaban de la orilla de mis labios
que comenzaban a dejar de ser palabra, verdad, luz,
ya era esa otra,
mientras mi cabello también se agrietaba, desteñida
entre las cenizas se dilataba como una flor mal parida
y desnuda los tenía que mirar

Torture

—For Rosa Montero and all those who told her their stories

Slowly and in secret
the roof of my silenced mouth burning
and I already naked and
so far away
conspiring to trap
my nipples, thin wires of terror.
Their small fingers, sloughed off scales of bitter wormwood
venture along that slow agony, through obscured
brightness between my legs
and they, the idle hangmen,
pant while
the moon's blood
howls on the sickly metal surface,
they wipe my forehead
so that later they can empty the
scattered leaves of mystery
and between gaps of time
seconds of air
electric spears and tears
explode like falling leaves of unhinged warriors
fingernails spread out over the floor in flames and menses,
teeth crushed by shocks and traitorous spittle
let go from the shore of my lips
now shorn of word, truth, light
now turned into something other,
even my hair splits, withers
among the ashes and fans out like doomed petals
naked I am forced to face

a cada uno de ellos,
tenía que confesarles
secretos que no poseía,
alojamientos inciertos
y ante cada silencio,
las mortajas negras como los brumos agrios
me enrollaban para
comer la lengua que no tenía que contar,
para destripar esa lengua
que antes sabía de pájaros, luces, de cebollas
en un jardín
y otra vez la tormenta de hilos rojizos envolviéndome como un
hilo de mal agüero, en los cimientos de mis pies, en mis
pechos hundidos por el pavor de sus
terribles garras verdes.
Ahora estoy muerta,
me llamo Carmen, o María,
soy una mujer
en medio de este silencio,
en medio de mi desnudez,
como una piedra
encarcelada,
soy una muerta que pudo sobrevivir
pero no contó nada
nuevo,
que perdidió en unos instantes los olores, las lilas, el amarillo,
porque durmió junto a otros cuerpos defecando, muriéndose
de pena y no de miedo,
soy esa que estuvo vendada por un segundo, por un mes
y para siempre
atravesada por la
ceremonia eterna de la
tortura.

each one of them
to confess to them
secrets I never had,
uncertain living places
and before each silence,
black shrouds like those of mordant warlocks
coil round me to
consume the tongue that had nothing to tell,
to strip the tongue
that once knew about birds, light and onions
in a garden
and again the torment of glowing wires weaving me in
threads of ill omen, the soles of my feet,
my breasts shrunken by the terror of the
terrible green talons.
Now I am dead,
my name is Carmen, or Maria,
I am a woman
immersed in silence,
immersed in my nakedness,
an imprisoned
stone,
I am a dead woman who managed to survive
who told nothing
new,
who in a matter of moments lost aromas, lilacs, yellow,
while sleeping next to other bodies defecating, dying
from pain and not from fear,
I am the woman who was blindfolded for a second, for a month
and forever
impaled by the
eternal ceremony of
torture.

El dios de los niños

–Para Elena Gascón-Vera

Mientras la desnudaban amarrándola
y con precisión de anfitriones y cirujanos
le preguntaron que en
que Dios cería
si en el de los moros o judíos
ella cabizbaja y tan lejana
repetía
yo creo en el Dios de los niños.

The God of Children

—For Elena Gascón-Vera

They undressed her and bound her
and speaking precisely as diplomats and surgeons
asked her
which God she believed in
that of the Moors or that of the Jews
head hanging and so far away
she kept saying
I believe in the God of children.

La Amordazada

Entre rendijas y amuletos,
sofocada por una brisa afilada,
la amordazada
pregunta
por esa mano
cercana al
epitafio,
por esa mano que
le trae un pan entre
los sollozos
y un agua anochecida.

La amordazada,
grita, con piedad
cuando esa mano
la golpea como si la
acariciara entre las maldades de la niebla
y esa mano de garza, cuchillo, o ave generosa
después de bofetadas y heridas,
la cubre de verdores y solitarios
epitafios.

The Shrouded Woman

Between slits and amulets,
suffocated by a whetted breeze
the shrouded woman
asks
for that hand
next to the
epitaph,
for that hand
that brings her bread among
sobs
and darkening water.

The shrouded woman
cries out with compassion
when that hand
strikes her as if it were
caressing her among the evils of the fog
and that hand of thorn, knife, or generous bird
after the blows and wounds,
covers her with greenish and solitary
epitaphs.

Ana Frank y nosotras

I.
Como una cicatriz
atada a las
dolencias de
la noche,
Ana Frank
me visita con frecuencia.

II.
Lleva lazos de ausencias,
a veces, lleva
mirada de lluvia y algas
y sus ojos se posan inquietos dentro
de los míos para que mi mirada
la sobreviva, la cuente
o la haga.

III.
Me pregunta María del Carmen
si conozco a todos mis muertos,
se me acerca diáfana o diabólica,
yo no puedo prometerle regresos,
ni descubrirle su mirada desvelada,
su mirada de dagas e insomnios.

IV.
Sonia de las Mercedes
me visita con frecuencia
mientras como, sueño amo o bebo
hay un eco de la muerte entre nosotras,
hay un eco de la vida
ente nosotras.

Anne Frank and Us

I.
Like a scar
attached to
the aches of
nighttime,
Anne Frank
visits me often.

II.
She comes bringing loops of absences,
at times she brings
a glance of rain and seaweed
and her eyes alight restively upon
my own so that my glance
will survive her, tell her
or be her.

III.
María del Carmen asks me
if I know all my dead,
she comes near me diaphanous or diabolical
and I can't promise her returnings
nor can I discern her wakeful glance,
her glance of daggers and sleeplessness.

IV.
Sonia de las Mercedes
often visits me
while I'm eating, dreaming, loving, or drinking
there's an echo of death between us,
there's an echo of life
between us.

V.

Cecilia Gabriela y yo
nos hemos hecho amigas
le cuento de mis sueños, las cenizas y las dichas de las palabras.
Ella me sonríe acusándome piadosamente.
Ella me sonríe para que le devuelva una mirada
para que la mire una y otra vez
muerta bajo las alambres del espanto.
Pero viva en la mirada que la sobrevive.

VI.

María Cecilia me visita.
A tí también te visita.
No podemos transfigurarla ni aniquilarla con
árboles muertos.

Ella es espléndida en su resplandor,
y en sus olores a muerte clausurada.

Ana Frank, María del Carmen, Sonia de las Mercedes,
Cecilia Gabriela, me despiertan en las noches
para pedirme
que no las olvide.

V.
Cecilia Gabriela and I
have become friends
I tell her my dreams, the ashes and happiness of words.
She smiles at me, accusingly, compassionately.
She smiles at me so that I'll return her glance,
keep looking at her again and again
dead beneath the wires of terror.
Alive in the glance that survives her.

VI.
María Cecilia visits me.
She visits you too.
We cannot transfigure her or annihilate her
with dead trees.

She is resplendent in her splendor,
in her aroma of cloistered death.

Anne Frank, María del Carmen, Sonia de las Mercedes,
Cecilia Gabriela, they all wake me up at night
to ask me
not to forget them.

Podríamos haber sido ella

Podríamos haber sido ella
of tal vez ¿era yo
ella?
Nacidas en el mes de los peces
treinta y dos años de inocencia
y de terror.
Judías desnudas persequidas
podriámos haber sido todas
nosotras ellas?

Vendadas en celdas de suspiros y demencias
plasmadas por el olor a heridas
a jadeos en la oscuridad de
una noche que gime.

Me podrían haber cortado mis pechos
y con la sangre construir un trofeo
de fuegos calcinados.

Me podrían haber cortado
mi cabello
amordazar mis visiones.

Me salvé.
Sobreviví.

Esta vez no vinieron por mí
aunque con zapatillas los esperaba.

Yo ya no tengo respuestas
pude ser ella
esa Alicia vendada abierta y calada.

Could We Have Been Her?

Could we have been her
or perhaps I was
her?
Born in the month of the fish
thirty-two years of innocence
and terror.
Naked persecuted Jewish women—
could all of us have been
them?

Blindfolded in cells of sighs and dementia
molded by odor of wounds
gasping in the darkness of
a night that howls.

They could have cut off my breasts
and used the blood to make a trophy
of calcined fires.

They could have cut off
my hair
muzzled my visions.
I saved myself.
Survived.

This time they didn't come for me
although, wearing my slippers, I waited for them.

Now I have no answers
I could be her
that Alicia blindfolded laid open torn apart.

No fui
pero tal vez sí fui ella.

Y ahora ¿vendrán por tí
en las noches de los huesos que brillan?

I wasn't
but then perhaps I was her.

And now will they come for you
on a night of glittering bones?

La desparecida

Soy la desaparecida,
en un país anochecido,
sellado por los
iracundos anaqueles
de los desmemoriados.¿ Aún no me ves? ¿Aún no me oyes
en esos peregrinajes
por las humareadas
del espanto?
Mírame,
noches, días, mañanas insondables,
cántame
para que nadie me
amenace
llámame
para recuperar
el nombre,
los sonidos,
la espesura de la piel
nombrándome.

No conspires con
el olvido,
derriba al silencio.
Quiero ser
la aparecida
y entre los laberintos
regresar, volver
nombrarme.
Nómbrame.

Disappeared Woman

I am the disappeared woman,
in a country grown dark,
silenced by the
wrathful cubbyholes
of those with no memory.
You still don't see me?
You still don't hear me
in those peregrinations
through the dense smoke
of terror?
Look at me,
nights, days, soundless tomorrows
sing me
so that no one may
threaten me
call me
to give me back
name,
sounds,
a covering of skin
by naming me.

Don't conspire with oblivion,
tear down the silence.
I want to be
the appeared woman
from among the labyrinths
come back, return
name myself.
Call my name.

La desaparecida II

Y ahora que todos
desaparecieron
como chales malheridos
¿a quién buscarán
los verdugos?
¿qué haremos con
los torturadores
que pasean
con las
manos chamusqueadas
de sangre añeja?

Disappeared Woman II

Now with everybody
disappeared
like mutilated shawls
whom will they search for?
The executioners?
And what will we do with
the torturers
who walk about,
their hands
charred
by moldering blood?

La desaparecida III

Encontrarla,
      hallarla,
tenerla
aunque sea su cuerpo
una fábula mutilada,
un equinoccio de
heridas como leyendas.

Encontrarla.
Sentir su aliento.
Imaginarla.
Lejos de funerales e
infiernos.

Sujetarla
para enterrarla
como Dios manda
con su nombre apegado
a la greda
con flores
para su santo.

Disappeared Woman III

Find her,
        uncover her,
hold her
even though her body be
a mutilated fable,
an equinox of
wounds like legends.

Find her.
Feel her breath.
Imagine her.
Far from funerals and
infernos.

Bind her
to bury her
as God commands
with her name attached
to the clay
with flowers
on her Saint's Day.

La desaparecida IV

La sueño a orillas del camino,
a orillas de un mar intermitente.
Lleva piedras sin inscripciones
bajo su manta de cielo,
y su pelo coagulado
abandonó la miel de
antiquos presagios.

Viene entre sus chales de
sol y sombra,
lleva golondrinas en
sus bolsillos
y migas violetas
como faros,
iluminando
el sendero
de sus antepasados.

La sueño entre mis tinieblas
llena de la vida,
los espectros de la mala muerte
revolotean,
como los monstruos, los captores,
pero yo la oigo
y en los umbrales
la abrazo.

Disappeared Woman IV

I dream her by roadsides
by the shores of an intermittent sea.
She carries stones with no inscriptions
beneath her cloak of sky
and her clotted hair
has left behind the sweetness of
ancient omens.

She comes wrapped in shawls of
sun and shadow,
carrying swallows in
her pockets
and violet-colored crumbs
like beacons illuminating
the path
of her ancestors.

During my dark hours I dream her
full of life
specters of evil death
are fluttering round her,
like the monsters, the captors,
but I hear her
and on thresholds
I embrace her.

La desaparecida V

Yo no tuve testigos
para mi muerte.
Nadie elaboró sacrilegios y epitafios.
Nadie se acercó para una despedida
oscurecida.

A mi entierro,
no se pudo asistir
porque el silencio de la incertidumbre
cubrió un cuerpo desvanecido, des-encontrado
asomándose pérfido entre las neblinas.

Las autoridades,
me han desmentido.
No aparezco en los huesudos murmullos de la morgue.
No existo en los cardexes.
Nadie me vió alejarme trastocada de mi país.
Nadie plantó nombres bajo mis plantas.

Soy una extraviada,
una mano fugándose y maldecida.
Soy de lluvia y de granadas
y cuando me nombran me
aparezco
porque a mi entierro
nunca fuí.

Disappeared Woman V

I had no witnesses
to my death.
Nobody carried out rituals, wrote epitaphs.
Nobody came near
for a veiled
farewell.

No one could come
to my burial
because the silence of uncertainty
covered a body disappeared, dis-encountered
rising up treacherous amid the mists.

The authorities
have concealed me.
I do not appear among the morgue's murmuring bones.
I don't exist in the Cardex files.
Nobody saw me, transmuted, leaving my country.
Nobody put numbers on the soles of my feet.

I am a stray,
a hand fleeing and accursed.
I am made of rain and grenades
and when they call my name
I will appear
because I never went to my
own funeral.

La desaparecida VI

Madre mía
sé que me llamas
y que tus yemas
cubren esas heridas, abiertas
muertas y resucitadas
una y otra vez.

Cuando vendada
me llevan a los
cuartos del
delirio.
Es tu voz
nueva,
iluminada,
que oigo
tras los golpes
desangrados
como los árboles
de un
patio de
verdugos.

Madre mía
yo duermo entre
tus brazos
y me asusto
ante los puñales
pero
tú me recoges
desde un fondo
lleno de dagas y serpientes.

Disappeared Woman VI

Mother
I know you are calling me
and that your fingertips
are covering those wounds, open
dead and re-opened
over and over again.

When I am blindfolded
they carry me to the
rooms of
delirium.
It is your voice
new,
luminous,
that I hear
after the bloodletting
blows
like trees
in a
patio of
assassins.

Mother
I sleep in
your arms
and feel frightened
by the knives
but
you gather me up
from the abyss
filled with daggers and serpents.

Memorial de las locas en la Plaza de Mayo

–A la memoria de Marta Traba

No hay nada aquí,
la plaza, en silencios,
diminuta, azulada,
entre los cirios que se despliegan
como ajenos bultos
revolcándose,
encima de las piedras.

¿Hay alguien aquí?
Comienzan las peregrinaciones de las transparentes,
las procesiones,
las palabras de las ilusas,
son, dicen,
las locas de la Plaza de Mayo,
en busca de ojos,
de manos tibias,
en busca de un cuerpo,
de tus labios para jamás poseerte
para siempre llamarte
amado.

Agrietadas, enjutas,
orando,
gritando de rabia,
preguntando
encima de los bultos
más allá de los ecos,
las locas,
en Buenos Aires, El Salvador,

Remembering the Madwomen of the Plaza de Mayo

—In memory of Marta Traba

There is nothing here,
the plaza, silent,
small, blue,
in the center of candles that fan out
like alien shapes
circling
over the stones.

Is there anyone here?
It begins, the pilgrimage of the invisible ones
the procession,
the words of the deluded women,
they are, it is said,
the madwomen of the Plaza de Mayo,
searching for eyes,
for warm hands,
searching for a body,
for your lips, not to possess you
but so I can always call you
beloved.

Wrinkled, skeletal,
praying,
screaming in rage,
questioning
above the shapes
beyond the echoes,
the madwomen,
in Buenos Aires, in El Salvador,

en Treblinka
quieren saber
necesitan saber,
¿dónde están los hijos de los diecisiete?
¿los padres-esposos?
¿los novios de las más niñas?
¿acaso son los arrojados al río maloliente de los justos?
Se acercan,
míralas como vuelan las brujas de la verdad
míralas como la lluvia arrastra sus lánguidos y demenciales cabellos,
mírales los pies, tan pequeños para arrastrar el dolor del abandono,
el dolor de la indiferencia.

Las locas,
amarrando la fotografía demolida, arrugada, borroneada, vacía de la memo-
ria incierta
la fotografía cautiva
¿por quién? ¿para quién?
mira el silencio en la plaza de las locas, mira como la tierra se esconde,
se enmudece,
se revuelca como una muerta herida que sólo
quiere descansar,
y es sólo silencio quien acude a oírlas,
es el silencio
de la plaza
quien oye
las fotografías
de los olvidados
presentes.

in Treblinka
want to know,
have to know,
where are their seventeen-year-old sons?
their husbands, fathers of their children?
the boyfriends of the youngest girls?
were they perhaps thrown into the fetid river of their judges?

They come near,
look at them how they flutter, the witches of truth,
look at them how the rain plasters down their listless and demented hair
look at their feet, how small they are to bear the pain of abandonment,
the pain of indifference.

The madwomen
holding fast to a photograph, tattered, wrinkled, faded,
empty of uncertain memory
captive photograph
by whom? for whom?
look at the silence in the plaza of the madwomen, look how the earth
scurries to hide,
tires,
falls back like one mortally wounded who only
wishes for rest,
and so it is only silence that comes to hear them
it is the silence
of the plaza
that listens to the photographs
of the forgotten ones
here present.

Delantales de humo

Abismada y llena de pesadumbres
aladas,
la sangre se extiende,
danza y recorre el
delantal de humo,
se traslada hasta el
comienzo de mis
piernas y
enloquecida no me obedece,
sólo rueda destemplada
invade los colores
de mi piel
me trastorna de
carmesí...
y entre el pavor del silencio,
entre la lejanía del
espanto,
se apodera de mis muertos y de mis vivos
marchita se despide
robándome a un niño
muerto
perdido entre los coágulos de mareas envenenadas.

Aprons of Smoke

Somber and full of winged
nightmares,
blood spreads out,
dances and overruns the
apron of smoke,
moves to the
edge of my legs and
maddened does not obey me,
but flows untimely
invades the colors
of my skin
deranges me with
crimson...
and between the horror of silence
the distance of
terror,
takes possession of my dead and my living ones
faded takes leave
robbing me of a child
dead
lost among clots of venomous tides.

Desnudas en los bosques de alambre

I.

A veces me disfrazaba de sacerdotiza, dando saltos por el aire.

A veces visitábamos prostíbulos y lavábamos sus paredes con hojas de rosa cobriza.

A veces jugamos a mirarnos, a ver las olas en la brisa.

La verdad era incierta. Las sirenas de las alarmas estables, seguras.

Entonces tu y yo nos queríamos con una especie de perversa y censurada locura. Gozaba en desnudarte, enredarte en una bufanda de lana picante, morder las dimunutas y sinceras uñas, llenar tu espalda de miel, dejar que las estaciones, los osos, limpien las desjuiciadas heridas del amor.

—Tú esperabas el momento preciso para cortar mi cabello de princesa rusa; teñirlo de algas venenosas que conservabas a la orilla de tus pies. A veces, me golpeabas las manos, ceremonioso, como un anciano languideciendo. Yo desmayada fingía soñar en tus cabellos y tú entrabas desfrenado por las líneas de mis palmas.

Como un mago seguro, espléndido en las caricias, decías: No te salvarás hasta que nos desnudemos y exploremos las manchas oscuras del cielo razo.

II.

Nos queríamos entre los indicios y los gestos, entre las uvas de la medianoche y las ropas amontonadas en esa casa deshabitada. Dudosos entre las palabras nos llamábamos en secreto con frenesí de delicada pornografía. Dejó de ser todo. Todas las promesas entre las orejas y las señales abiertas de los lasios cuando me dijiste: Desnúdate judía ya ahora, frápido, ya desnúdate, ya tendrás plata para hacerte el remedio.

III.

En la ilusoria tibieza del cuarto, entre los girasoles y las mantas de lana, sobre las sábanas envestidas de mareas, llegaron por las murallas, asediaron los inmensos espacios, se alzaron por el volcán de leños, las desnudas judías de los bosques espesos en Dachau, Treblinka, Baden-Baden, las

Naked Girls in the Forests of Barbed Wire

I.

At times I dressed up as a priestess, and went leaping through air.
At times we visited houses of prostitution and washed the walls
      with coppery leaves.
At times we played games of staring at one another, of seeing waves in the
      breezes.
Truth was uncertain. The sirens of the alarms stable, secure. Then you
and I loved each other with a kind of perverse and censorious madness. I
loved to take off your clothes, wrap you in a prickly woolen shawl, nibble
your tiny and sincere nails, spread honey over your shoulder and let the
seasons, the bears clean the unthinking wounds of love.
—You waited for the precise moment to shear my hair of a Russian
princess; to stain it with the venomous seaweed you always kept at the
shore of your feet. At times you would slap my hands ceremoniously like a
courtly old gentleman. I, trancelike, would pretend to sleep in your hair,
and you would burst wantonly through the lines of my palms.
Like a confident sorcerer, splendid in caresses, you said: You can't escape
until we take off our clothes and explore all the dark splotches of the ceiling.

II.

We loved each other with signs and gestures, amid grapes at midnight and
piled clothes in that uninhabited house. Not trusting words, we called out
to each other covertly, in a frenzy of delicate pornography. Suddenly it all
ceased to be. All the promises between the ears and the clear language of
the lips when you said to me: Strip naked Jew girl right now, quick, strip
naked hurry, you'll be taken care of if anything happens.

III.

Streaming into the illusory warmth of the room they come, drift among
the sunflowers and the woolen covers, hover over sheets blessed with sea
breezes, invade through the walls, besiege the immense space, erupt

desvaliddas judías en la neblina humeante. Desveladas por un bosque de
arios reptiles olfateando los pechos, las nalgas. El cuerpo de una judía des-
tilada por los bosques de alambre.

IV.
Judías desnudas,
 indefinidas, en silencio
judías dando gritos de fe a hurtadillas, cerrando piernas, labios con la
dignidad milenaria de los ilusos, estatuas de humo apresuradas hacia las
duchas de gas azul, duchas oscuras con sabor a viñedos enfermizos.

V.
Judías desnudas
sobrevivientes, desaparecidas gravitando entre tus rodillas, regresando por
el bosque de los alambres. Retornando al cuarto de los hallazgos
demenciales, plasmado de ratas crepitando en una hoguera, bañada en la
muerte oscura, precisa. Tú pareces que crepitas en ese fuego, mientras los
verdugos se curbren de premeditadas sonrisas para observar un cuerpo
esencial: una desnuda mujer judía, dormida con un tatuaje entre sus piernas.

VI.
Era cierto que tal vez nunca nos supimos mirar.

through the volcano of tree trunks, the naked Jewish girls from the thick forests of Dachau, Treblinka, Baden-Baden, defenseless Jewish girls coming through the smoky fog. Defenseless before a forest of Aryan serpents slithering over breasts, buttocks. The body of one Jewish girl distilled from the forests of barbed wire.

IV.
Naked Jewish girls
nameless, silent
Jewish girls contriving to call out words of faith, closing legs and lips with the ancient dignity of the innocent,
statues of smoke hurried into showers of blue gas, black showers with the taste of sickly vineyards.

V.
Naked Jewish girls
the survivors, the vanished ones sinking down heavily between your knees, come back from the forests of barbed wire. Come back to the place of demented discoveries, machination of rats, crackling bonfire, bathed in death, black, exact. You too seem to crackle in that fire, while the hang-men paste premeditated smiles on their faces the better to see an elemental body: a naked Jewish woman asleep, tattoo between the legs.

VI.
Clear that never had we known how to see ourselves.

Las Piezas Oscuras

La oscuridad se guarda
en las ranuras del miedo.
No distingo los ojos
que me miran.
¿A quién corresponde
la voz
que no me nombra
y transita sobre mis
palmas que sudan que
tiemblan que ya no aman?

La oscuridad se
estrecha cada vez más
como un sollozo dolido,
soy una niña que
tiene miedo
y en esta oscuridad sólo
hay vendados y verdugos.

No he tratado de cooperar
con las tinieblas,
y por eso
me azotan,
me olvidan
y navego descuartizada
en la pieza oscura l
lejana, borrosa, delirante.

The Dark Rooms

Darkness waits for me
in the interstices of fear.
I can't make out the eyes
looking at me.
Who owns the
voice that does not name me
and passes over my palms that sweat
and tremble
that no longer love?

The darkness tightens
more and more,
like a painful sob,
I am a child
afraid
and in this darkness only
blindfolds and hangmen exist.

I have not tried to cooperate
with the darkness,
and for that
they flog me
forget me
and I float disjointed
in the dark room
distant, blurred, delirious.

¿Cómo ve una prisonera a la luz?

La prisionera en el umbral
sueña con la luz
la insinúa rodeándola
entre los nombres y las
claridades que
traspasan colores.
Juega con la luz
insaciable, matinal y colorida
mientras despierta a
los que se aman
reclamando la memoria
de las hogueras.

Ella pide un trozo de luz
reclama la luz para
no olvidar las manos extendidas
abiertas libres de insomnios y crímenes
la luz para desmadejarse, unirse a sus cabellos
a la textura de sus brazos agrietados.

La prisionera en el umbral
sueña con la luz
y ensombrecida entre las vendas
y oscurecida en las celdas cómplices
silba por la luz
inventa un trozo de oro
entre los qujlidos.

How Does an Imprisoned Woman See the Light?

The imprisoned woman on the threshold
dreams of the light
senses it surrounding her
along with names and
clearings that
go beyond colors.
She plays with the light
insatiable, morning-like and many-colored
while rousing
those who love one another
calling up a memory
of bonfires.

She asks for a sliver of light
demands light so as
not to forget hands extended
open free of sleeplessness and crimes
light to become languid, to mingle with her hair
the texture of her fissured arms.

The prisoner on the threshold
dreams of the light
and sombered among blindfolds
obscured in complicitious cells
she summons up the light
invents a sliver of gold
in the midst of laments.

La prisonera y la luz

La luz como débil rehén,
se alza rojiza, espectacular,
nocturna tras los orificios
delgados de una ciudadela
sin mar.

Desde las recámaras,
donde se ofician
ceremonias de magia negra,
y el amor es un feto solapado entre
las llanuras,
la luz se me acerca,
trepa hasta mi cuello
y en sus caricias
me voy haciendo un solo espejo entre los espejos
de la muerte.

Ausente me palpo,
ya nadie late dentro de mí,
no tengo rostros ni escrituras.
Comienzo a reconocerme dentro de esta
ausencia deforme
como un árbol estancado oculto entre verdes falsos.

La luz persiste en
enseñarme, a ver desde esos ojos
prohibidos, desde esa venda sajada y sucia de tiempos y cristales solos.

The Captive Woman and the Light

The light like a feeble hostage
rises rosy, spectacular,
nocturnal behind narrow
breaches of a fortress
without a sea.

From the cots
where ceremonies of
black magic take place
and love is a furtive fetus between
the flatness,
the light approaches me,
creeps to my throat
and in its caresses
I turn into a lone mirror among the mirrors
of death.

Absently I feel myself,
now nobody throbs inside me,
I possess neither faces nor writings.
I begin to recognize myself within this
ill-formed absence,
like a stunted tree hidden among false greens.

The light persists in
teaching me to see from these forbidden
eyes, from the blindfold slashed and sullied from lonely times and prisms.

La prisonera y la luz II

Soy una sombra visitada
entre los colores
desaparecidos.
Soy un crepúsculo
que borra mis huesos
desalmados.

La luz me pide que la
quiera
y comienzo a estirar mis ojos en el umbral de los quejidos,
me destapo,
magentas, amarillos, rosas, rosados
me visten en un solo enjambre de
vestidos sanos.

Comienzo a ser y ver colores,
la sombra deja de cubrirme,
y grandes tajadas de amarillos
laten entre mis dedos
y grandes tules de púrpuras visiones
me rodean.

El sol se asemeja a un gran durazno alucinado,
piso cuidadosamente la luz entre el umbral y un pasado
agazapado.
La luz me invade perteneciéndome
y el sol me convida su piel de fiestas.
Comienzo a mirar.
Aprendo a verme.

The Captive Woman and the Light II

I am a shadow visiting
among disappeared
colors.
I am a dawn
erasing my soulless
bones.

The light asks me to
love her
and I begin to move my eyes on the threshold of laments,
I throw off the cover,
magentas, yellows, pinks, rosiness
clothe me in a single host of
healthy clothes.

I begin to be and to see colors,
the shadow no longer covers me,
and thick slabs of yellow
pulse between my fingers
and great webs of purple visions
surround me.

The sun resembles an enormous raving peach,
I step carefully on the light between the doorsill and a past
in ambush.
The light invades me, belongs to me,
and the sun offers me its festive skin.
I begin to look.
I learn to see myself.

Pupilas

La luz desbordada y melódica
franquea los corredores de
mis pupilas selladas.
Imagino verdores, la espesura
del mar abierto, noble en su
excelsa profundidad.
Invento escamas y peces
vahos y espumas
de buenos vientos.

Te busco entre las
desformidades.
Fabrico tus manos de harina,
juego que jugamos a deslizarnos
entre las arenas, entre los
relojes del tiempo ingrato.

Yo vendada te reconozco,
oigo entre las vendas sombrías
que me llamas,
y es tu voz
una zona de muertes
una llaga que anida
entre las tristezas.

Pupils

Light overflowing and melodious
breaches the corridors of
my sealed pupils.
I conjure up greens, the generous
open sea, noble in its
sublime depths.
I invent scales and fish
mist and spume
of fair winds.

I look for you among the
misshapen.
I fabricate your hands fine as flour,
play that we are playing at slipping away
across the sands, eluding the
clocks of a bitter time.

Blindfold or not I recognize you,
among the shadowy masks I hear
you calling me,
and your voice is
a zone of deaths
a wound that makes its nest
amid the sadness.

Los ojos de los enterrados

Los ojos de los enterrados,
como en una lejanía inquieta,
nos amenazan
oyélos, oyéme.

El que sobrevive,
en letanías de
memorias prestadas
se estremece, se verifica
porque tan sólo los muertos-moribundos
transfigurados por los sabores del olvido
pueden aparecer,
cautivándonos en esa memoria-mirada que acecha.

Ahí estás Ana Frank,
entre inocente y pérfida
comiéndonos mientras te miramos.
Tú eres los ojos de los enterrados.
Y nos devuelves esa mirada
cadavérica o diabólica.

Ahí estás Milena tan abandonada con la estrella de David cubriéndote
como látigo o promesa.

Ahí estás Lila Valdenegro. Desaparecida. Carnet 353, olvidada en la memo-
ria que no desmiente.
Los ojos de los enterrados
nos acusan
se acusan,
escribo, me miran
y me atraviesan
las ausencias.

The Eyes of the Interred

The eyes of the interred,
as in a restless distance,
threaten us
listen to them, listen to me.

The survivor,
in litanies of
borrowed memories
trembles, inspects himself
because only the dead-dying
transfigured by the savors of oblivion
may appear,
capturing us in that backglance-foreglimpse lying in wait.

There you are Anne Frank,
between innocent and devious
devouring us as we look at you.
You are the eyes of the interred.
And you send us back that glance
cadaverous or diabolical.

There you are Milena so abandoned with the Star of David covering you
like a lash or promise.

There you are Lila Valdenegro. Disappeared. I.D. number 353, forgotten
in a memory that does not deny.
The eyes of the interred
accuse us,
accuse themselves,
I write, they watch me
and the absences
transfix me.

¿Que hay en el fondo de tus ojos?

-Para Guillermo Núñez

¿Qué hay en el fondo
de tus ojos?
¿Cuándo te vendan?
¿Cuámndo la luz es una trenza de pájaros amorfos?

En el fondo de tus ojos,
la duermevela,
el sol cómplice y generoso,
la ondulación del aire,
las estaciones itinerantes,
el amarillo colorido resguardándose
en las aceras azules.

En el fondo de tus ojos,
mientras la oscuridad transcurre por sus contornos,
y la venda es una incierta enfermera manca,
estás tú
porque eres de luz
porque eres una encendida mariposa en los espejos.

What Lies in the Depths of Your Eyes?

–Para Guillermo Núñez

What lies in the depths
of your eyes?
When they blindfold you?
When the light is a braid of amorphous birds?

In the depths of your eyes,
half-sleep,
complicitous and generous sun,
undulating air,
wandering seasons,
yellows sheltering
in blue facades.

In the depths of your eyes,
the sea, rivers transformed into
caresses
into the roundness of living children.

In the depths of your eyes,
while darkness courses over their contours,
and blindfold is a dubious maimed nurse,
you are there
because you are made of light
because you are a butterfly luminous in the mirrors.

Desde la celda perfilo el rastro

Anochecida perfilo rastros:
la memoria como una crónica
destemplada
me acaricia y entre las
sombras, inventa una guirnalda
con el nombre de los bienamados.

Los huéspedes de mi celda sonríen
y mi madre ensangrentada me
revuelve los cabellos
en una ofrenda de duendes y magas.

Inútil encarcelada,
no me canso en llamarlos
y la voz se desata entre los
huesos de mi piel.

Anochecida, anochece.
No hay luces ni días
en mi celda.
Nadie me reconoce en esta lejanía,
pero ellos, los huéspedes
no me olvidan
y en sus gestos
soy.

From the Cell I Outline the Trace

Darkened I outline traces:
memory like an out-of-tune
chronicle
caresses me and amid the
shadows, concocts a garland
of the names of my loved ones.

Visitors to my cell smile at me
and my mother all bloody
ruffles my hair
in an offering of spirits and sorcery.

Useless imprisonment,
I don't grow tired calling them
and my voice breaks loose between the
bones of my skin.

Darkened, I grow dark.
There are neither lights nor days
in my cell.
Nobody recognizes me in this desolation,
but they, the visitors,
don't forget me
in their gestures
I exist.

Entre los pinos

Una luz ahorcada atraviesa los pinos. La niebla desfigurada con sus alfombras de brumas se desliza entre las hiedras rasuradas. Alguien, ilumina las lámparas del aire frío. Alguien anda buscándome para ahorcarme entre los prismas de la luz.

La luz como una ahorcada en medias de sedas y musgo, me vigila. Sueño que me ahorcan. Me ahorcan porque sueño. Mi cabeza es una orgía desparramada para los ojos de los enterrados.

Yo no tengo miedo. Conozco al que ahorca. Bajo un extraño gozo, lo espero. Pero alguien me desliza, me trepa alejándome fuera de esta vigilia.

El olor de pinos se encuentra. El encierro me aleja de las ternuras.
Y el olor de la ahorcada se arrastra bajo el hundido pavimento.

Among the Pines

A gallows light traverses the pines. The disfigured fog with its brumous carpets slips over the close-cut ivy. Someone lights the lamps of the cold air. Someone goes in search of me to hang me among the prisms of the light.

The light like a hanged woman in stockings of silk and moss watches me. I dream they hang me. They hang me because I dream. My head is an orgy spread for the eyes of the interred.

I am not afraid. I know who does the hanging. Feeling a strange pleasure, I await him. But someone slips me away, lifts me, takes me far from this vigil.

The scent of pines is present. The enclosure severs me from all tenderness. And the odor of the hanged woman drags itself along beneath the sunken paving stones.

La sangre es un nido

La sangre es un nido de plumas,
adornando la invalidez de las
sábanas.
Yo sobreviví.
No tengo respuestas.
Las preguntas quedaron
en mi huida.

The blood is a nest

The blood is a nest of feathers
adorning the nullity of the
sheets.
I survived.
I have no answers.
The questions stayed behind
in my flight.

Más que la paz

Más que las paz
o la alegría
pido un colchón
de hojas
de otoño
para reposar
entre la sombra
inventar solsticios
coloridos
transfigurarme en esa suave
manta de hojas secas
amarillas
siempre vivas.

No quiero nombres
ni tumbas
para mis muertos
ni compartir cementerios
con huesos
extraviados
sólo denme
mi colchón
de hojas
sólo déjenme
regresar a mis
bosques.

More Than Peace

More than peace
or joy
I ask for a pillow
of autumn
leaves
in order to rest
among the shadows
to invent solstices
of many colors
transform myself in that smooth
mantle of dry leaves
yellow
everlasting.

I want neither names
nor tombs
for my deaths
nor to share cemeteries
with bones
gone astray
just give me
my pillow
of leaves
just let me
go back to my
forests.

Nos acogió

Nos acogió
la claridad
formando una
sonrisa en
el claro
del bosque.

Tu cabeza
como una colina
se rodeó de
pétalos.
Te rociaron de lluvia.

Ya nadie nos podría detener
en las travesías sedosas como
labios esparciendo decires,
porque rodó la luz
como una ronda
de niños
como unas voces
de girasoles.

Todo, hondo y bello
y el claro de la
luz
alumbrándonos.

We Were Met

We were met by
a clarity
forming a
smile in
a clearing
in the woods.

Your head
like a hill
was ringed with
petals.
They sprinkled you with rain.

Now nobody could hold us back
in crossings silky as
lips scattering sayings,
because the light rolled
like a child's hoop
like the speech
of sunflowers.

All, deep and beautiful
and the clear
light
bringing us to light.

The Author

Marjorie Agosín is well-known as poet, writer, critic, and human rights activist. Editor of White Pine Press' acclaimed Secret Weavers Series: Writing by Latin American Women, she is a professor at Wellesley College in Wellesley, Massachusetts. Her published titles include *Ashes of Revolt, Happiness, A Cross and A Star: Memoirs of a Jewish Girl in Chile, Melodious Women, Women in Disguise,* and *Dear Anne Frank.*

The Translators

Celeste Kostopulos-Cooperman is director of the Latin American studies program at Suffolk University, Boston, Massachusetts. Her book *The Lyrical Vision of María Luisa Bombal,* was published by Tamesis Press in London, and her translations of Latin American women writers and poets have appeared extensively. She won the ALTA Prize in 1993 for her translation of Marjorie Agosín's *Circles of Madness.*

Cola Franzen is a well-known and widely-published translator. She resides in Cambridge, Massachusetts. Her translation of Marjorie Agosín's *Zones of Pain* was a finalist for the *Los Angeles Times* Book Award. She also translated Agosín's *Sargasso,* which was published by White Pine Press in 1993.

Mary Guyer Berg is well-known as both translator and critic. She holds M.A. and Ph.D. degrees from Harvard University, where she presently lectures in the history and literature programs. Her work has appeared in numerous anthologies and magazines. Her translation of *Latin America in Its Literature* was published in 1980, and White Pine Press published her tranlation of *Starry Night,* poems by Marjorie Agosín in 1996.

THE WHITE PINE PRESS HUMAN RIGHTS SERIES

*A continuing series dedicated to discussing and revealing
human rights issues around the world.*

The United Nations stated in its landmark Declaration of Human Rights that all people have the right to personal freedom and that no one should be detained unlawfully or tortured for any purpose. Although the human rights regulations set up by the United Nations have been adopted and upheld in most countries, in others human rights abuses have been allowed to flourish, making torture and disappearance a fear that many people face in everyday life. In most cases it is a corrupt government or military system that commits these crimes against humanity, wishing to silence those who do not uphold the ideals of the ruling force and who are subsequently seen as subversive.

The issues surrounding human rights need to be brought to the political forefront if we are to stop human rights abuses around the world, but unfortunately, the main stream media in the United States gives these issues little attention. That there is tremendous interest in these issues is clearly demonstrated by the fact that the first three volumes in the series, *Circles of Madness, Surviving Beyond Fear,* and *From the Republic of Conscience,* sold out their entire print runs.

The White Pine Press Human Rights Series tackles issues of human rights from a variety of perspectives and formats. While some volumes rely on the traditional essay and testimony to convey information, other volumes take the creative forms of poetry, art, and fiction. Traditionally, writers have been at the forefront of human rights movements in many countries and have often been imprisoned, tortured, censored, exiled, and suffered death because of their words. It is the intention of the series that these voices be heard.

White Pine Press has a long-term commitment to the Human Rights Series and plans to publish at least one volume per year. We have planned a variety of promotions for each of our human rights titles including author tours, workshops, and traveling photo exhibits (when applicable). In addition, Amnesty International is supporting the series and will make our titles available to Amnesty members through their newsletter.

To continue this important work, it is imperative that White Pine Press, a not-for-profit publisher, find additional funding sources. Underwriting of the publication costs including production, promotion, and translation of the Human Rights Series is available to foundation, corporate, and individual sponsors. Donations are tax deductible For further information on how you can help in this important cause, please call or write the press. Our address, e-mail address, telephone, and fax numbers are listed on the copyright page.

Ashes of Revolt
Essays on Human Rights
Marjorie Agosin
Volume 4   ISBN 1-877727-56-3   184 pages $15.00 paper

Ashes of Revolt collects a wide range of essays on human rights, writers, artists, and places in Latin America. Ms. Agosin is a native of Chile and is currently a professor of Spanish at Wellesley University in Wellesley MA. The essays have been published in a wide variety of journals including *American Voice*, *Human Rights Quarterly*, and *The Harvard Review*. The topics of the essays include notes on the "disenchanted generation," Latin American cities, women and human rights, memory and forgetting, the dictator in Latin American novels, as well as essays on writers, artists, and activists including Pablo Neruda, Anne Frank, Alicia Partnoy, Delfina Nahuenhual, Alaide Foppa, and Julietta Kirkwood.

Ms. Agosin is an accomplished writer and poet, having published many works which focus on the trouble in her native land and on the human rights abuses that have taken place throughout Latin America. Her books of poetry include *Circles of Madness, Zones of Pain, Bonfires, Women of Smoke* and *Sargasso*. Her non-fiction works include *A Cross and a Star, Scraps of Life* and *The Mothers of the Plaza de Mayo*. She has also published book of fiction, *Happiness and Other Stories*. She is the editor of White Pine Press' Secret Weavers Series, which brings writing by Latin American women t the English-speaking audience..

"...she writes knowingly about the vast differences between Latin American culture and ours and how it affects our world view...Agosin does her best with her essay on literature and human rights which, as opposed to technical writings on the subject, exposes the the most, and the least, noble aspects of the human spirit."

—Louise Leonard, *Counterpoise*

Heart's Agony
Selected Poems of Chiha Kim
Translated by Won-Chung Kim and James Han
Volume 5   ISBN 1-877727-84-9   128 pages $14.00 paper

First imprisoned in 1964, Chiha Kim was sentenced to death in 1974. His crime: writing poetry that provoked the military dictatorship of

Chunghee Park in Korea. Worldwide efforts to save him were begun in Japan, and he was released in 1980, after the assassination of Park. Winner of the prestigious Lotus Prize, Kim is a legendary figure in Asia. This book gathers poetry from all phases of his work, including poems that led to his repeated imprisonment and torture, poetry written in prison, and his post-prison poetry, which reflects the inter-connectivity of all life.

An Absence of Shadows
Poems by Marjorie Agosín
Volume 6   ISBN 1-877727-92-X   224 pages $15.00 paper

To celebrate the fiftieth anniversary of the United Nations Declaration of Human Rights, White Pine Press has combined two volumes of Marjorie Agosín's most enduring books of poetry, *Zones of Pain* and *Circles of Madness: Mothers of the Plaza de Mayo*, both of which are out of print, into one, bilingual volume. Additionally, the volume contains a large section of new work, updating these important human rights issues and acknowledging that the United States needs to address human rights abuses within its own borders.

Heart of Darkness
Poems of Ferida Durakovic
Edited by Greg Simon
Translated by Amela Simic & Zoran Mutic
Foreword by Christopher Merrill
Volume 7   ISBN 1-877727-91-1   112 pages $14.00

Durakovic lived in Sarajevo during the war and seige, and her poems reflect the reality of that experience.

Ferida Durakovic is secretary of the PEN Center of Bosnia-Herzegovina in Sarajevo. She is the author of five collections of poetry including *A Masked Ball* (1977), *Eyes That Watch Me* (1982) and *Little Night Lamp* (1989). In addition, she has published two children's books: *Another Fairy Tale About the Rose*, and *The Eccentric Dark*. Christopher Merrill is the author of *Watch Fire*, a collection of poetry, and the editor of *The Four Questions of Melancholy: Selected Poems of Tomaz Salamun*, a finalist for the *Los Angeles Times* Book Prize for poetry. He lives in Connecticut and is presently writing a book on the Balkans. Amela Simic is an author and translator living in exile in Toronto, Canada. Zoran Mutic lives in Sarajevo, where he translates work both fromand into English and Greek.

About White Pine Press

Established in 1973, White Pine Press is a non-profit publishing house dedicated to enriching our literary heritage; promoting cultural awareness, understanding, and respect; and, through literature, addressing social and human rights issues. This mission is accomplished by discovering, producing, and marketing to a diverse circle of readers exceptional works of poetry, fiction, non-fiction, and literature in translation from around the world. Through White Pine Press, authors' voices reach out across cultural, ethnic, and gender boundaries to educate and to entertain.

To insure that these voices are heard as widely as possible, White Pine Press arranges author reading tours and speaking engagements at various colleges, universities, organizations, and bookstores throughout the country. White Pine Press works with colleges and public schools to enrich curricula and promotes discussion in the media. Through these efforts, literature extends beyond the books to make a difference in a rapidly changing world.

As a non-profit organization, White Pine Press depends on support from individuals, foundations, and government agencies to bring you important work that would not be published by profit-driven publishing houses. Our grateful thanks to the many individuals who support this effort as Friends of White Pine Press and to the following organizations: Amter Foundation, Ford Foundation, Korean Culture and Arts Foundation, Lannan Foundation, Lila Wallace-Reader's Digest Fund, Margaret L. Wendt Foundation, Mellon Foundation, National Endowment for the Arts, New York State Council on the Arts, Trubar Foundation, Witter Bynner Foundation, the Slovenian Ministry of Culture, The U.S.-Mexico Fund for Culture, and Wellesley College.

Please support White Pine Press' efforts to present voices that promote cultural awareness and increase understanding and respect among diverse populations of the world. Tax-deductible donations can be made to:

White Pine Press
10 Village Square • Fredonia, NY 14063

Volume 5
A GABRIELA MISTRAL READER
Translated by Maria Giacchetti
232 pages $15.00

Volume 3
LANDSCAPES OF A NEW LAND
Short Fiction by Latin American Women
194 pages $12.00

Volume 1
ALFONSINA STORNI: SELECTED POEMS
Edited by Marion Freeman
72 pages $8.00 paper